4/15

Mayan, Incan, and Aztec Civilizations

Author: Michael Kramme, Ph.D.

Editors: Mary Dieterich and Sarah M. Anderson

Proofreader: Margaret Brown

COPYRIGHT © 2012 Mark Twain Media, Inc.

ISBN 978-1-58037-629-7

Printing No. CD-404162

Mark Twain Media, Inc., Publishers
Distributed by Carson-Dellosa Publishing LLC

Visit us at www.carsondellosa.com

Table of Contents

Introduction

Mayan, Incan, and Aztec Civilizations provides resources for the study of the major Indian civilizations of Central and South America. The mysteries and differences in culture of these civilizations can easily catch the imagination and natural curiosity of today's students.

Each civilization has a general survey chapter. The lesser-known civilizations such as the Olmecs and the Toltecs have only one or two chapters. A series of specialized narrations follow the survey chapter for the major civilizations (Maya, Inca, and Aztec). However, each narrative may stand independently of the survey chapter.

This book is specifically designed to facilitate planning for the diverse learning styles and skills levels of middle-school students. The special features of the book provide the teacher with alternative methods of instruction. Teachers may choose to use the readings as class projects or as extra enrichment activities for individual students. The activities are designed for students to complete individually. Suggestions for group projects have been included. A modified version of the text is available for download for struggling readers.

Book Features:
- **<u>Reading Selection</u>** introduces facts and information as a reading exercise.
- **<u>Knowledge Check</u>** assesses student understanding of the reading exercise using selected response and constructed response questioning strategies.
- **<u>Map Follow-Up</u>** provides opportunities for students to report information from a spatial perspective.
- **<u>Explore</u>** allows students to expand learning by participating in high-interest, hands-on and research activities.

Online Resources:

Reluctant Reader Text: A modified version of the reading exercise pages can be downloaded from the website at www.carsondellosa.com. In the Search box, enter the product code CD-404162. When you reach the *Mayan, Incan, and Aztec Civilizations* product page, click the Resources or Downloads tab. Then click on the Lower Reading Level Text Download.

The readability level of the text has been modified to facilitate struggling readers. The Flesch-Kincaid Readability formula, which is built into Microsoft® Word™, was used to determine the readability level. The formula calculates the number of words, syllables, and sentences in each paragraph, producing a reading level.

Additional Resources:

Classroom decoratives appeal to visual learners. The *Mayan, Incan, and Aztec Civilizations* Bulletin Board Set, available from Mark Twain Media, Inc., can be used to visually reinforce lessons found in this book in an interesting and attention-grabbing way. The *Seven Continents of the World* Bulletin Board Set and the *Continents of the World* Mini Bulletin Board Set may also be helpful when studying the geography of these civilizations.

Time Line

B.C.

before 8000	Man crosses the Bering Strait into the Americas
8000	Land bridge covered by Bering Sea as ice caps melt
2500	Pre-classical Period of the Mayas
1200	Beginning of the Olmec civilization (Peak of culture 700 to 400)
200	Altiplano Indians begin building city of Teotihuacan
100	Olmec civilization disappears

A.D.

250–900	Mayan Classical Period
600	Olmec and Altiplano city of Teotihuacan reaches its peak
750	Teotihuacan destroyed
900–1200	Toltec civilization
900	Mayas abandon their cities; Post-classical Period
1100	Incan city of Cuzco founded
1150	Toltec city of Tula destroyed
1200	Aztecs begin to settle in the Valley of Mexico
1325	Aztecs found city of Tenochtitlan
1438–1471	Reign of great Incan ruler Pachacutec
1440–1468	Reign of great Aztec ruler Montezuma I
1492	Columbus discovers the Americas
1502	Columbus meets Mayan traders
1519	Montezuma II captured
1521–1525	Cortés defeats Aztecs
1533	Incan ruler Atahualpa is defeated by Spanish under Pizarro and is killed
1697	Tayasal, the last Mayan kingdom, falls to the Spanish
1790	Discovery of the Aztec calendar stone
1911	Incan city of Machu Picchu is rediscovered

The Arrival of Man

Crossing the Bering Strait Land Bridge

Giant ice caps covered both the Arctic and Antarctic regions of the earth over 50,000 years ago. The levels of the oceans lowered because much of the earth's water was trapped in the **polar ice caps.** The lower water level exposed a piece of land that connected Siberia to Alaska. Today this area is once again under water and is called the Bering Strait. Many scientists believe that early humans crossed over this land bridge and began to spread out and settle in what is now North America. These people then moved into Central and South America. The **Bering Strait land bridge** disappeared under the water when the ice caps thawed. This happened at the end of the Ice Age around 8,000 B.C.

Today, we refer to the first people who settled in the Western Hemisphere as **Paleo-Indians** or Paleo-Americans. *Paleo* is a prefix from the Greek language meaning "old." The term *Indian* comes from the time of Columbus' voyages when he thought he had landed in India. Other names for native people include Native Americans and First Nations. Each tribe or cultural group has its own name for its people.

As tribes migrated throughout North, Central, and South America, they discovered agriculture and learned how to make stone tools and clay pottery.

Hunting and Gathering

The Paleo-Indians were hunters and gatherers. All of their food came from plants, animals, and fish located near where they lived. When the food supplies ran out, the people moved on to another area to find a fresh supply. These people had to move constantly to find enough food.

Discovering Agriculture

No one knows who made the discovery of **agriculture.** This was one of the most important discoveries ever made by humans. Their way of living changed forever when they learned to plant and harvest crops. This allowed them to remain in one area for longer periods of time. Since they no longer had to move to find food, they built permanent villages. Huts made of mud and branches provided housing for these early tribes.

Making Pottery

Paleo-Indians also discovered how to form clay and bake it to make pottery, which helped them store grain from the harvests. At first, craftsmen made pottery only to store food. They later decorated their vessels to look attractive as well as to be useful.

Studying How Ancient People Lived

Scientists called **archeologists** must solve many puzzles to find out how the Paleo-Indians lived. Ancient garbage dumps can give important information about foods that were eaten. Remains of stone spearheads, arrowheads, and tools can also give clues to solving the puzzles. Stones used to grind grain and bits of broken pottery tell us about early agriculture. Scientists make new discoveries each year. Each new discovery helps us to better understand how the Paleo-Indians lived.

Name: _____ Date: _____

Knowledge Check

Matching

_____ 1. polar ice caps
_____ 2. Bering Strait land bridge
_____ 3. Paleo-Indians
_____ 4. agriculture
_____ 5. archeologists

a. an exposed piece of land that once connected Siberia to Alaska
b. water frozen in the Arctic and Antarctic regions
c. scientists who study the lives of ancient humans
d. planting and harvesting crops and raising livestock
e. the first people to settle in what is now North, Central, and South America

Multiple Choice

6. What two ways did the Paleo-Indians first get their food?
   a. planting
   b. gathering
   c. hunting
   d. manufacturing

7. Why was the water level of the oceans lower during the Ice Age?
   a. the ice caps thawed
   b. there was very little rain
   c. water was frozen in ice caps
   d. water had shifted to the Southern Hemisphere

8. What did the Paleo-Indians use to make the buildings in the first villages?
   a. mud and branches
   b. wooden boards
   c. bricks and mortar
   d. cement

9. Why was pottery first made?
   a. for decoration
   b. to use as hats
   c. to hold ashes
   d. to store food

Constructed Response

10. How can archeologists find out about the lives of the Paleo-Indians? Use details from the reading selection to help support your answer.

_____

_____

_____

_____

_____

_____

_____

Name: _____ Date: _____

Map Follow-Up

Using a globe or world map to help, write the names of the following locations on the map below.

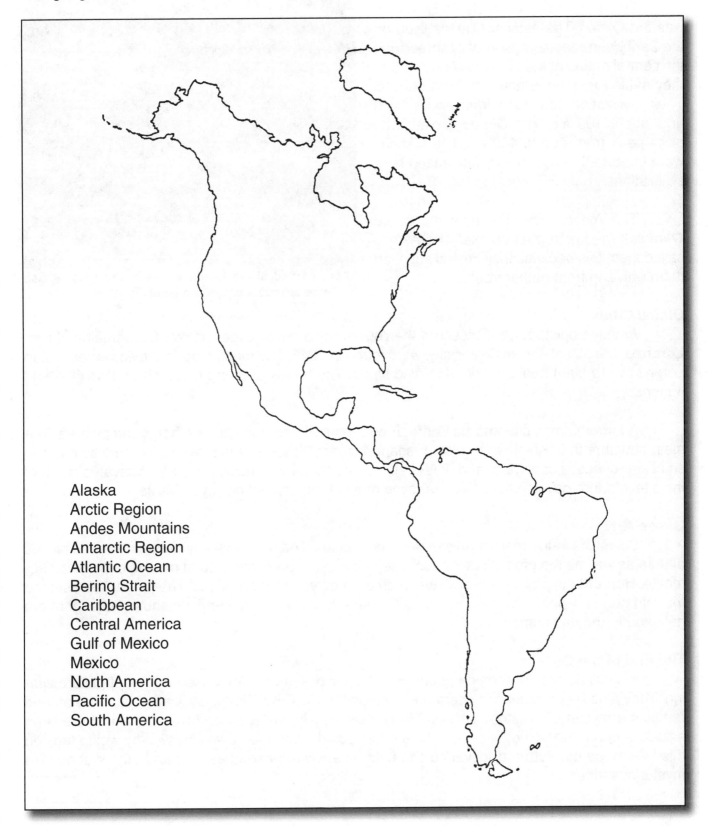

Alaska
Arctic Region
Andes Mountains
Antarctic Region
Atlantic Ocean
Bering Strait
Caribbean
Central America
Gulf of Mexico
Mexico
North America
Pacific Ocean
South America

The Olmecs

The Olmecs in Mexico

The first major tribe of Central America was the Olmec. The earliest Olmecs lived on the Caribbean coast and eventually spread into the central region of the Valley of Mexico. Later they settled in what is now southern Mexico. Their civilization continued from about 1200 until about 100 B.C. The Olmec society was at its peak from 700 to 400 B.C. The Olmecs were important because they influenced later civilizations.

The Aztecs gave the tribe the name *Olmec*. It means "rubber people." The Aztecs called them this because the Olmecs supplied them with sap from rubber trees.

Giant carved stone heads found in the area of San Lorenzo are ruins of the Olmec civilization.

Olmec Cities

Archaeologists have discovered the **ruins** of two major Olmec cities. The remains of **San Lorenzo**, the oldest known Olmec city, were found in 1945. The most important discoveries in San Lorenzo were giant heads made of carved stone. The heads are nine feet high and weigh about 40 tons.

A larger Olmec city was **La Venta**. It was located on an island in a hot, swampy area. The main structure in La Venta is a volcano-shaped pyramid over 110 feet tall. La Venta also has two smaller mounds, a courtyard, and other painted structures. Scientists have not excavated much of the site. Modern development has destroyed most of the ancient city of La Venta.

Olmec Art

Scientists found many works of art in both cities. The artworks include small carved pieces of jade as well as the giant stone heads. They also found perfectly ground mirrors of polished hematite. **Hematite** is a glass-like substance created by volcanic eruptions. The jaguar represented the rain god and was a favorite subject of Olmec art. Many Olmec carvings show figures that are half jaguar and half human.

The End of the Olmecs

We still do not know much about the Olmecs' daily lives. They used a form of picture writing. They also had a number system and a calendar. How the Olmec civilization came to an end remains a mystery. The stone carvings were deliberately smashed and then buried. There is no evidence of an invasion of enemies. Did the Olmecs destroy their own cities? Why would they do this? We hope that future discoveries can help us answer these questions and others about this mysterious tribe.

Name: _____ Date: _____

Knowledge Check

Matching

_____ 1. Olmec

_____ 2. ruins

_____ 3. San Lorenzo

_____ 4. La Venta

_____ 5. hematite

a. name that means "rubber people"; they lived in central and southern Mexico

b. Olmec city with a volcano-shaped pyramid

c. the remains of something that has been destroyed

d. glass-like substance created by volcanic eruptions

e. oldest known Olmec city where giant stone heads were found

Multiple Choice

6. What animal represented the rain god for the Olmecs?

    a. elephant

    b. lizard

    c. jaguar

    d. python

7. Who gave the Olmecs their name?

    a. the Aztecs

    b. the Mayas

    c. archeologists

    d. Mexicans

8. What did the Olmecs make out of hematite?

    a. bowls

    b. mirrors

    c. combs

    d. calendars

9. Where did the first Olmecs live?

    a. the central Valley of Mexico

    b. southern Mexico

    c. the Pacific coast of Mexico

    d. the Caribbean coast of Mexico

Constructed Response

10. Name at least three things we know about the Olmecs' daily lives. Use details from the reading selection to help support your answer.

_____

_____

_____

_____

_____

_____

_____

Teotihuacan

The Altiplano

Teotihuacan is an ancient city located near Mexico City. It began about 200 B.C. and reached its peak around A.D. 600. People known as the **Altiplano** built Teotihuacan. The Olmec influenced the Altiplano, and many people believe the Altiplano tribe descended from the Olmec tribe. Teotihuacan became the capital of the Altiplano tribe. It once had a population of over 100,000 people.

The most famous structure in the Altiplano city of Teotihuacan is the Pyramid of the Sun

The Altiplano worshipped gods similar to those of the Olmecs. Both tribes used picture writing called **glyphs**. They also played similar ritual ball games. Both tribes traveled and traded goods over great distances.

Teotihuacan

The city of Teotihuacan covered over eight square miles. It had pyramids, temples, palaces, markets, and a variety of shops and houses. One unusual thing about the city was its many apartment buildings. Most ancient cities had only single-family houses.

The Altiplano people planned Teotihuacan very carefully. Its structures were all built on a grid plan. The main road, named the **Avenue of the Dead**, connected three of the main temples. There are four well-known buildings in Teotihuacan. The most famous structure in the city is the **Pyramid of the Sun**, which is 200 feet tall. It is as large at the base as the great pyramid in Egypt. Another important structure is the smaller **Pyramid of the Moon**. The **Temple of Quetzalcoatl** is also an important building in the city. It is named for a serpent god. Carvings of serpents and a god named Tlaloc cover the walls of the temple. The other major building in the city is the **Temple of the Jaguars**. It is famous for its brightly colored wall murals.

The Mystery of Teotihuacan

The history of this ancient city remains a mystery. We do not have any written records of the time. The ruins have not provided much information about the beliefs or daily lives of the people. We do know that they made a special thin orange pottery. Examples of this pottery have been found throughout Mexico, so we know that the Altiplano traveled and traded over great distances.

Mystery shrouds the last days of Teotihuacan. About A.D. 750, the entire city was destroyed and burned. The ancient temples and carvings were smashed. Some historians believe outside tribes invaded and destroyed the city. Other historians assume the priests and rulers destroyed their own city. We may never know the answer.

Teotihuacan means "the place where men become gods." Centuries after the destruction of the city, the Aztecs believed the gods had built Teotihuacan. The Aztecs worshipped it as a holy site.

Name: _____ Date: _____

Knowledge Check

Matching

_____ 1. Temple of the Jaguars

_____ 2. Temple of Quetzalcoatl

_____ 3. Pyramid of the Sun

_____ 4. Pyramid of the Moon

_____ 5. Altiplano

_____ 6. Avenue of the Dead

_____ 7. glyphs

_____ 8. Teotihuacan

a. the main road in Teotihuacan

b. people believed to be descended from the Olmecs

c. picture writing

d. the capital of the Altiplano tribe

e. named for a serpent god

f. most famous structure in Teotihuacan

g. famous for its brightly colored wall murals

h. smaller pyramid found in Teotihuacan

Multiple Choice

9. Who did the Aztecs believe had built Teotihuacan?

   a. the Olmecs

   c. the Altiplano

   b. the gods

   d. ancient Aztecs

10. What present-day city is the ancient city of Teotihuacan near?

    a. Veracruz

    c. Mexico City

    b. Lima

    d. Acapulco

Constructed Response

11. How do we know that the people of Teotihuacan traveled a great deal? Give details from the reading selection to support your answer.

_____

_____

_____

_____

_____

_____

_____

_____

The Mayas

The Territory of the Mayas

The Mayan culture spread throughout southern Mexico and Central America. It included the **Yucatan Peninsula** to the north as well as today's countries of Honduras, Belize, El Salvador, and Guatemala to the south. It stretched from the Pacific Ocean in the west to the Caribbean Sea in the east. This land included rugged highlands as well as dense swamps.

The Mayan People

The Mayan people were short. The average height of the men was just over five feet. The women were about four feet eight inches tall. Mayas had straight black hair, and many painted their bodies black, red, or blue. They also often had tattoos. They valued crossed eyes and tied objects from their infants' foreheads to encourage their eyes to cross. Some Mayas also tied boards to the heads of their children to flatten their foreheads.

Mayan History

Historians divide the story of the **Mayas** into three eras: the pre-classic, the classic, and the post-classic. The **pre-classic era** lasted from about 2,500 B.C. to A.D. 250. During this time, the Mayas came in contact with and borrowed from the Olmecs. The early Mayan settlements were fishing villages along the Pacific Ocean and Caribbean Sea; they moved inland when they learned to plant crops.

The Mayas created sculptures on large stone slabs called stela. These carvings reveal much about the Mayan people.

The Mayan **classic era** continued from A.D. 250 to A.D. 900. They built many great cities, most of which had majestic pyramid temples. **Tikal**, the largest Mayan city, may have had a population of 100,000 or more. During the classic era, the Mayas improved methods of agriculture. They also developed advanced mathematics and astronomy as well as a system of writing.

The **post-classic era** began with the collapse of the Mayan empire after A.D. 900. It lasted until the **Spanish conquest** in the 1500s. One of the world's greatest mysteries is what happened to the Mayan culture. It was the most important civilization in the new world in A.D. 900. Suddenly, however, the Mayas left their great cities and scattered throughout the countryside. We still do not know why the great Mayan civilization ended. The Mayas continued to farm and trade in the region after the great cities fell. Christopher Columbus met some Mayan traders in 1502. Mayan descendants still live in the region of their ancestors.

Name: _____   Date: _____

Knowledge Check

Matching

_____ 1. Yucatan Peninsula

_____ 2. Mayas

_____ 3. pre-classic era

_____ 4. classic era

_____ 5. post-classic era

_____ 6. Tikal

_____ 7. Spanish Conquest

a. period when the Mayas built many great cities

b. time when soldiers from Spain conquered the natives of the new world

c. the largest Mayan city

d. people who lived in the Yucatan Peninsula and what is today Belize, El Salvador, Honduras, and Guatemala

e. period when the Mayas lived in fishing villages

f. period after the collapse of the Mayan empire

g. area of land that juts out into the Caribbean Sea; includes part of Mexico, Belize, and Guatemala

Multiple Choice

8. What was one trait Mayan people did not have?

    a. straight hair

    b. tattoos

    c. tall

    d. crossed eyes

9. What allowed the Mayas to move inland?

    a. they found fish in streams

    b. they learned to plant crops

    c. they began hunting

    d. they found an Olmec city

10. What were the most well-known structures in Mayan cities?

    a. burial mounds

    b. deep wells

    c. level roads

    d. pyramid temples

Constructed Response

11. What evidence is there that the Mayas had an advanced civilization? Use details from the reading selection to help support your answer.

_____

_____

_____

_____

_____

_____

_____

Name: _____ Date: _____

Map Follow-Up

The shaded area of the map below shows the ancient Mayan empire and the Mayan cities of Chichén Itzá, Tikal, and Copán. Use a globe or atlas and write in the names of the modern locations listed.

Belize
Mexico
El Salvador
Nicaragua

Gulf of Mexico
Caribbean Sea
Yucatan Peninsula

Honduras
Pacific Ocean
Guatemala

The Mayan Empire

Mayan Religion

Religion was important to every part of Mayan life. The Mayas worshipped many different gods. Each day, month, city, and occupation had its own special god or goddess. The Mayas had a variety of religious festivals and celebrations. Most of these celebrations included human sacrifice.

Each Mayan city-state had a ruler called the halach uinic. He may have also served as the high priest during religious ceremonies.

Halach Uinic: Ruler and Priest

The Mayan empire was divided into many city-states. Each city-state had its own ruler. His name was *halach uinic*. This meant "the true or real man." The Mayas believed halach uinic was a living god. He ruled until his death. At his death, his oldest son became the next halach uinic. If the halach uinic did not have a son, his brother would rule. If he did not have a brother, the ruler's council elected a member of his family to serve. Some historians believe that the halach uinic also served as the high priest during religious ceremonies.

The halach uinic dressed in elaborate and colorful clothes. He also wore a very large headdress. Temple wall paintings show him with large ear decorations, crossed eyes, and many tattoos.

Mayan Priests

Many other priests served with the halach uinic. These priests, named *ahkin,* performed many duties. They had the knowledge of mathematics and astronomy. Some of the ahkin were prophets. Some of them performed the religious sacrifices. Other ahkin performed medical rituals. The Mayas believed that only the priests could explain the mysteries of life and death. The Mayas believed that the earth was flat. They thought it was on the back of a crocodile that floated in a large pond. At another time they believed the earth was the floor of a lizard house.

Heaven, Earth, and the Underworld

The Mayas' religion taught that there were 13 layers of heavens above the earth. They also believed nine underworlds were below. They thought that they lived in the fifth creation of the world. The previous four worlds had each been destroyed by a great flood. At the beginning of the fifth world, the gods created humans from corn.

Sacrifices to the Gods

Many of the Mayan religious ceremonies included gifts and sacrifices to the various gods and goddesses. The Mayas believed the gods would give favors to them in return for prayers, offerings, and sacrifices. The **sacrifices** included valuable gifts, their own blood, and human sacrifices.

In many ceremonies, the priests cut themselves to get blood to present to the gods. The Mayas had three methods of giving the human sacrifices. Often, the priests took the victim to the altar at the temple. Then the priests cut the heart out of the living victim and presented it to the god. In another method, the priests tied the victim to a wooden pole. Then they threw spears and arrows at the victim's chest in the area of the heart. In the third type of sacrifice, they threw the victim into a sacred well. The most famous of these wells is the Well of Sacrifice at Chichén Itzá. If victims survived the fall and did not drown, the priests pulled them back out of the well. The Mayas believed the gods had chosen to spare these victims. The priests then asked the victims what messages they brought back from the gods. The victims received special treatment from then on since the Mayas believed they had spoken to the gods.

Worshipping the Dead

The Mayas also worshipped the dead. They believed the dead became one with the gods. They worshipped their ancestors at many religious ceremonies. They also built pyramids over the sacred remains of their dead rulers.

The Mayan Gods and Goddesses

The Mayas worshipped many gods. Here are some of the more important ones:

Itzamná: He was the head god, lord of the heavens and lord of night and day. His name meant lizard. Carved pictures show him as an old crossed-eyed man. He had a lizard's body. The Mayas believed he invented books and writing.

Kinich Ahau: He was the sun god. He was also the god of the rulers.

Chac: He was the rain god. Carvings show him as a reptile with a large nose pointing down and curling fangs. He had four aspects:

Chac Xib Chac	Red Chac of the East
Sac Xib Chac	White Chac of the North
Ek Xib Chac	Black Chac of the West
Kan Xib Chac	Yellow Chac of the South

The Mayan Gods and Goddesses (cont.)

Yun Kaax: He is the god of maize (corn). He is also the god of all agriculture. Pictures always show him as a young man. He is either carrying a plant or has a plant as a headdress.

Ah Puch: He is the god of death. Carvings of him show a skull and skeleton.

Ek Chaub: He is the god of trade. Mayan artists painted his face black and he had a drooping lower lip.

Ix Chel: She is the moon and rainbow goddess. She is also the goddess of weaving and childbirth.

Buluc Chabtan: He is the god of war and human sacrifice. Carvings of him show a black line around his eye and down onto his cheek. He is at times shown with a torch or weapon in his hand.

Name: _____ Date: _____

Knowledge Check

Matching

_____ 1. halach uinic

_____ 2. ahkin

_____ 3. sacrifices

_____ 4. Itzamná

_____ 5. Chac

_____ 6. Yun Kaax

_____ 7. Ix Chel

a. the god of maize (corn)

b. the goddess of the moon and rainbow

c. the head god; lord of the heavens and night and day

d. the god of rain

e. ruler of a Mayan city-state; also may have been a high priest

f. things given to the gods, such as valuable gifts, their own blood, or other humans

g. Mayan priests who had knowledge of mathematics and astronomy

Multiple Choice

8. According to the Mayan religion, from what were humans made?

   a. crocodiles

   c. corn

   b. rain

   d. stars

9. Who was the Mayan god of death?

   a. Ah Puch

   c. Kinich Ahau

   b. Buluc Chabtan

   d. Ek Chaub

10. How many layers of heavens did the Mayas believe were above the earth?

   a. 5

   c. 11

   b. 9

   d. 13

Constructed Response

11. What would happen to a sacrificed person who did not die after being thrown into the sacred well? Use details from the reading selection to help support your answer.

_____

_____

_____

_____

_____

_____

_____

Mayan Cities

The ruins of Mayan cities remained hidden for centuries in the dense jungles. Scientists are still working to uncover and study most of these cities, but visitors can now explore the ruins of Tikal, Copán, Chichén Itzá, and several other cities.

The Pyramid of Kukulcan at Chichén Itzá

How Mayan Cities Were Organized

At first, scientists thought these locations were religious centers only. After further study, they found these were complete cities. The ceremonial center formed the heart of each city. Tall pyramids topped with temples stood in large open **plazas**, and public buildings, palaces, and **ball courts** surrounded the plazas.

The rulers and priests likely lived in the city's center. The upper- and middle-class citizens built their homes just outside the city center, and the peasants lived in huts on the edges. Raised roads, called **causeways**, ran through the city. Mayas built the causeways two to four feet above ground level. Some causeways measured up to 15 feet wide.

Construction Materials and Methods

The Mayas used carved stone for the main buildings of the city. They carved the giant building stones with simple tools that were also made of stone, since they did not have metal tools. They moved the stones to the building location using man power. They did not use animals or wheeled vehicles to help. A cement made of limestone provided mortar between the stones. The Mayas spread a limestone stucco or cement over stones to give the buildings smooth surfaces and then painted the buildings with bright colors.

Tikal

Tikal, in northern Guatemala, is the largest and perhaps oldest Mayan city. It spread over 50 square miles. Tikal's population may have reached over 100,000 people. The central plaza in Tikal measures 250 by 400 feet. Two of the eight pyramid temples of Tikal face each other across the great plaza. The temple of the Giant Jaguar and its pyramid rise over 150 feet. Scientists discovered a tomb inside one of the pyramids. There they found jade, pearl, and shell jewelry. Inscriptions revealed that it was a tomb containing the skeleton of a ruler named Double Comb.

Copán

Copán is the second largest Mayan city. It has five main plazas. The most famous ruin in Copán is the great staircase. It is 30 feet wide and has 63 steps. Picture writing covers each step. Copán also has a perfect example of a ball court.

Chichén Itzá

The ruins of **Chichén Itzá** include several plazas, pyramid temples, and ball courts. The great pyramid of Chichén Itzá is visible from miles away. An important ruin is the large observatory tower used by ancient astronomers. Chichén Itzá is the location of **The Well of Sacrifice**. The Mayas threw many live men into the well as sacrifices to the gods.

Name: _____ Date: _____

Knowledge Check

Matching

_____ 1. plaza

_____ 2. ball court

_____ 3. causeway

_____ 4. Tikal

_____ 5. Copán

_____ 6. Chichén Itzá

_____ 7. The Well of Sacrifice

a. largest and perhaps oldest Mayan city

b. ruins of this city include a great pyramid, observatory tower, and a sacred well

c. a raised road two to four feet above ground level

d. an open area in a city for public use

e. second largest Mayan city

f. place where Mayans played a game that has similarities to modern basketball, soccer, and football

g. place where live men were thrown to please the gods

Multiple Choice

8. Mayan tools were made of what material?

    a. iron

    c. bronze

    b. stone

    d. steel

9. Astronomers used what structure in Chichén Itzá for their work?

    a. observatory

    c. plaza

    b. pyramid temple

    d. ball court

10. Picture writing covers what famous ruin in Copán?

    a. Giant Jaguar temple

    c. observatory tower

    b. The Well of Sacrifice

    d. giant staircase

Constructed Response

11. Describe how a Mayan city was organized. Use details from the reading selection to help support your answer.

_____

_____

_____

_____

_____

_____

_____

_____

Mayan Writing

Glyphs

The Mayas used the most advanced system of writing of the ancient Americans. They probably borrowed the idea of picture writing from the Olmecs. They then developed their own system of writing based on that.

They did not use an **alphabet**. Instead, they used a combination of pictures to represent ideas and symbols to represent sounds. The pictures and symbols used in their writing are called **glyphs**. The Mayas combined glyphs into groups. These groupings have a square or oval shape. We know of about 800 different glyphs.

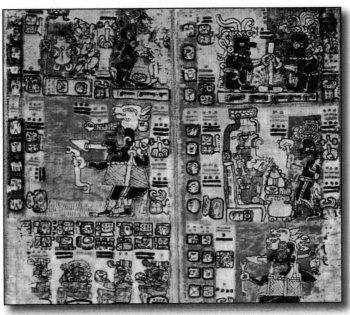

These are pages from the Mayan Codex in Madrid, one of the few remaining samples of Mayan writing.

Understanding the Glyphs

Scientists study Mayan writing in the few remaining Mayan books and examples carved on stones. Many of these stones are from ancient Mayan buildings. Scientists know the meaning of some of the Mayan symbols. Much of the Mayan writing system still remains a mystery. So far, we know the meaning of fewer than half the glyphs discovered.

Here are some examples of Mayan glyphs:

fish   vulture   dog   wife   death

Paper and Books

The Mayas had a process for making paper that used fibers from the bark of the **ficus tree**. They pounded the fibers into a **pulp** then glued the pulp together with tree sap. When the paper dried, they coated it with white lime. This made a smooth, white surface on which to paint.

The Mayas also made books. The name for a Mayan book is **codex**. Mayas used ficus-fiber paper or deer hide for pages. The pages of Mayan books folded from side to side and unfolded like a screen. They painted colorful glyphs and pictures of gods, animals, and objects on the pages of the codex. The Mayas used decorated boards for covers.

Spanish conquerors found great collections of Mayan books, but according to the beliefs of the Spanish, Mayan books were evil, so the conquerors destroyed most of them. Only three complete Mayan books survive today. They are located in museums in Europe. Only fragments of other Mayan books remain.

Name: _____ Date: _____

Knowledge Check

Matching

_____ 1. alphabet

_____ 2. glyphs

_____ 3. ficus tree

_____ 4. pulp

_____ 5. codex

a. tree fibers pounded into a soft mass that, when dried, forms paper

b. a writing system where each character stands for a letter

c. a writing system where pictures and symbols represent ideas and sounds

d. the name for a Mayan book

e. the Mayas used fibers from the bark of this plant to make paper

Multiple Choice

6. What did the Mayas use to make their paper white?

    a. tree bark   b. glyphs

    c. tree sap   d. lime

7. How many complete Mayan books still exist today?

    a. 3   b. 5

    c. 11   d. 16

8. Where do scientists get many of the samples of Mayan writing that they study?

    a. letters written by the Mayans   b. books in the Mexican national library

    c. stones from Mayan buildings   d. paintings in caves

Constructed Response

9. Why did the Spanish destroy Mayan books? Give details from the reading selection to support your answer.

_____

_____

_____

_____

_____

Mayan Mathematics and Astronomy

Mathematics

The Mayas developed an important system of mathematics. It was more advanced than the systems used by the ancient Egyptians, Greeks, or Romans.

Zero and Other Numbers

The Mayas were perhaps the first people to use the idea of a **zero**. This was an important

The Mayas built observatories in many of their cities to aid in their study of astronomy. This observatory in Chichén Itzá still stands today.

invention. They used a picture of a shell to equal zero. They also used a dot to equal one. A bar equaled five. The Mayas used a base of 20 the same way we use a base of ten. However, they wrote their numbers from top to bottom instead of from left to right as we do.

Mayan numbers looked like this:

| 0 | 4 | 7 | 10 | 13 | 19 |

Astronomy

An advanced system of **astronomy** was also developed by the Mayas. The priests studied the movements of the sun, moon, planets, and stars. They could predict **eclipses** and the orbit of the planet Venus. The Mayas believed that the heavenly bodies were gods. If they studied the sky, the Mayas hoped to learn to predict events on earth that these gods controlled.

To study the heavens, the Mayas built large **observatories** in many of their cities. The observatory at Chichén Itzá is one of the important Mayan buildings that still stands.

Calendars

The Mayan priests used their knowledge of astronomy and mathematics to develop accurate calendars. They had two different calendars. One was a sacred calendar, and the other was used for planning regular events.

The **sacred calendar** had 260 days. It used 20 day names, and each day had a god or goddess associated with it. They did not divide the sacred calendar into months. The Mayas used this calendar to determine religious events.

A **365-day calendar** based on the movement of the earth around the sun was also used. This calendar had 18 months of 20 days each. The Mayas believed the five extra days at the end of the year were unlucky. The Aztecs later based their calendar on that of the Mayas.

Name: _____ Date: _____

Knowledge Check

Matching

_____ 1. zero

_____ 2. astronomy

_____ 3. eclipse

_____ 4. observatory

_____ 5. sacred calendar

_____ 6. 365-day calendar

a. place where the Mayas studied the heavens

b. based on the movement of the earth around the sun; had 18 months of 20 days with five extra days at the end

c. studying the movements of the sun, moon, planets, and stars

d. had 260 days with 20 day names, each associated with a god or goddess; used to plan religious events

e. the idea of using a symbol to represent the absence of all quantity

f. when the sun or moon is blocked by another heavenly body and its light does not shine on earth

Multiple Choice

7. Mayas wrote their numbers from
   a. left to right.
   c. top to bottom.
   b. right to left.
   d. bottom to top.

8. What did the Mayas use to equal the number one?
   a. shell
   c. square
   b. dot
   d. bar

9. The Mayas' regular calendar had 18 months with 20 days each and five extra days at the end of the year. What was special about those five days?
   a. They were feast days.
   c. They were sacrifice days.
   b. They were lucky days.
   d. They were unlucky days.

Constructed Response

10. How did the Mayan priests use their knowledge of astronomy and mathematics? Use details from the reading selection to help support your answer.

_____

_____

_____

_____

_____

_____

Name: _____   Date: _____

Explore: Mayan Math Exercise

The Mayas used a shell to equal 0, a dot to equal one, and a bar to equal 5. Fill in the missing Mayan number symbols below.

| 0 | 1 | 2 | 3 | 4 | 5 | 6 |

| 7 | 8 | 9 | 10 | 11 | 12 | 13 |

| 14 | 15 | 16 | 17 | 18 | 19 |

Write in the answers to the following math problems, using Mayan numbers.

1. • •
    ―――
  + • • •
    ―――――

2. • • •
    ―――――
    ―――――
    ―――――
  − • •
    ―――――

3. • • •
  + • •
    ―――
    ―――
  + ⬮
    ――――――
  − ▬▬▬

4. • •
    ―――
  + • •
    ―――――
  − • • • •
    ―――――

On your own paper, make up and answer four Mayan math problems.

Mayan Arts and Crafts

Weaving

Nothing remains of ancient Mayan cloth, feather, or basket weaving. Due to the moist climate, all examples of these crafts have rotted away. Remaining pictures on murals, vase paintings, and sculptures show what these crafts looked like.

Only the Mayan women did the **spinning** and **weaving**. Cotton was the most common fiber used. At times, the women also wove rabbit fur fibers. They made cloth both for home use as well as something to trade for other objects.

Brightly colored cloth seems to be something the Mayas enjoyed. They used both minerals and vegetables to obtain **dyes**. Some colors had special meanings: black represented war, yellow symbolized food, red stood for blood, and blue indicated sacrifice.

The Mayas developed many brightly colored patterns to use in their weaving.

Many colorful birds living in the area supplied a variety of colorful feathers, and with these the Mayas did fancy featherwork. The Mayas used feather weaving to decorate clothing. They also made feather fans and headdresses.

The Mayas wove a variety of baskets from reeds, vines, rushes, and split cane. They also made rush mats and used them for floor coverings. Rope was another important product of the weavers.

Pottery

Numerous examples of Mayan **pottery** remain today since it does not decay. Shapes and decorations of pottery changed through the years. Scientists use pottery and broken pieces of pottery to decide the age of the piece. The Mayas did not use a potter's wheel. Instead, they made pottery from clay coils smoothed together. Cut-out molds were pressed onto the pots to create designs. Mayas made a great variety of pottery. Some pieces were as tall as an adult human.

Sculpture

Mayan **sculpture** has also lasted through time. Limestone was the most often used material for sculpture. Clay and wood carvings were used for decoration. The Mayas never developed metalwork. They used stone tools to carve. The most famous Mayan carvings appear on tall stones called *stela*. Stela still remain in the ruins of the Mayan cities.

Painting

Painting was another major Mayan artform. Scientists have discovered brightly colored **murals** on the walls of Mayan buildings. The murals are **frescoes**. The artists applied the paint while the walls were still wet. Mayan murals portrayed everyday scenes as well as religious ceremonies.

Name: _____ Date: _____

Knowledge Check

Matching

_____ 1. spinning

_____ 2. weaving

_____ 3. dyes

_____ 4. stela

_____ 5. fresco

a. substances that give color to cloth or other materials

b. forming cloth by interlacing strands of fiber, such as yarn, reeds, vines, or feathers

c. a carved stone slab

d. a painting done on a wall while the surface is still wet

e. twisting fiber into yarn or thread

Multiple Choice

6. What type of artform used coils of clay that were smoothed together to form pots?

    a. sculpture   b. painting

    c. pottery   d. weaving

7. In what type of artform is a hard substance like wood or limestone carved to make a statue or decoration?

    a. sculpture   b. painting

    c. pottery   d. weaving

8. What is a painting done on a wall called?

    a. portrait   b. miniature

    c. gallery   d. mural

9. What did the Mayas use to decorate clothing and make fans and headdresses?

    a. rabbit fur   b. feathers

    c. reeds   d. cotton

Constructed Response

10. List some of the colors used in Mayan weaving and what those colors represented to the Mayas. Use details from the reading selections to help support your answer.

_____

_____

_____

_____

_____

_____

Name: _____   Date: _____

Explore: Mayan Murals

Below are drawings of three of the murals from a temple in the Mayan city of Bonampok. On a large piece of paper, draw and color or paint a copy of one of the murals. You could also create your own mural in the style of Mayan art. Perhaps a bulletin board could be made of Mayan-style murals.

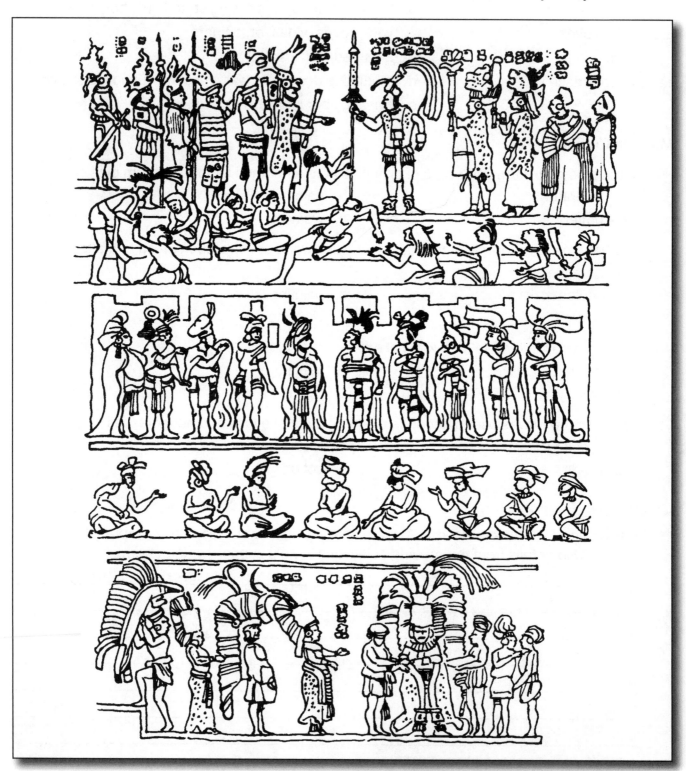

Mayan Agriculture

The Mayas used a variety of methods to obtain food. Which method they used depended on their location. For instance, methods used in the forest regions did not work in the swamps.

The slash and burn method of clearing land

Hunting and Gathering

The earliest Mayas were hunters and gatherers. They fished and hunted for food. Wild animals they hunted included birds, rabbits, monkeys, and deer. The Mayas also picked or gathered wild fruits, nuts, and vegetables. However, hunting and gathering alone could not provide enough food as the population increased. The Mayas then had to plant crops to survive.

Slash and Burn

A method known as **slash and burn** is one of the oldest methods of farming. Men cut forests down with stone axes and then let the trees dry thoroughly. The men then burned the dried trees to clear the land. The ashes provided **fertilizer** for the soil. The Mayas planted seeds, mainly **maize** or corn, using a planting stick. The farmers used the stick to make a hole in the soil and put three or four seeds into each hole. The slash and burn method wore out the soil quickly. The fields had to lie fallow, or at rest, for two or three years before replanting.

Chocolate was a delicacy throughout Central and South America. Cacao beans were often used as money.

Crops

Mayas raised a variety of crops. In addition to maize, they grew beans, chilis and other peppers, squashes, tomatoes, avocados, and pumpkins. In some regions at the edges of the empire, they grew **cacao** plants. The cacao plant was hard to grow, and its beans were valuable since they could be made into a Mayan delicacy called chocolate. The Mayas also had fruit orchards. In addition to food crops, Mayan farmers also grew hemp to make rope and cotton to make cloth.

Irrigation

Water for the crops was always a concern. Droughts often destroyed the crops. The Mayas built water reservoirs using man-made dams and created **irrigation** systems, but these were on a smaller scale than those of the Incas or Aztecs. They also built some terraces to help stop erosion.

The Mayas developed a special way of growing crops in the swampy areas. Workers dug soil up into mounds. They then planted and harvested the crops on the mound areas. The ditches they dug out provided **canals** around the mounds for irrigation.

Religion in Farming

Religion played an important part in Mayan farming. The priests chose the special days for planting and harvesting. The Mayas had special celebrations and rituals in honor of Chac, the god of rain. They believed that he would send the much-needed rain if the celebrations pleased him.

Name: _____ Date: _____

Knowledge Check

Matching

_____ 1. slash and burn

_____ 2. fertilizer

_____ 3. maize

_____ 4. cacao

_____ 5. irrigation

_____ 6. canal

a. plant whose beans are used to make chocolate

b. substance that makes soil more able to produce crops

c. a ditch that is dug to drain water either toward or away from an area

d. method of farming where trees are cut down and burned to clear land and provide fertilizer for the soil

e. another name for corn

f. bringing water to dry land

Multiple Choice

7. Who chose the days for planting and harvesting in Mayan farming?

    a. priests

    c. seed salesmen

    b. farmers

    d. gardeners

8. What did the Mayas use to help them plant corn?

    a. oxen

    c. plows

    b. axes

    d. sticks

9. Where did the Mayas plant their crops in swampy areas?

    a. on the riverbank

    c. on mounds of soil

    b. at the base of a tree

    d. on the side of a hill

Constructed Response

10. List some of the advantages and disadvantages of the slash and burn method of farming. Use details from the reading selection to help support your answer.

_____

_____

_____

_____

_____

_____

_____

Mayan Trade

Merchants

The Mayas became great traders. The Mayan name for merchants was **ppolm**. These ppolm became highly respected and important members of Mayan society. They even had their own god, Ek Chaub.

Trade Routes

Trade routes developed throughout the Mayan lands. Later, trade went as far south as Guatemala and Belize. Trade also extended to the Caribbean Islands.

The Mayas used large, seagoing canoes to carry on trade in the Gulf of Mexico and the Caribbean.

Human **caravans** carried the trading goods. The Mayas did not use animals or wheeled vehicles to move goods. Instead, slaves did most of the carrying.

In the interior, small pathways criss-crossed the land. The Mayas did not build major road systems, but they did build **canoes** for river travel. The rivers provided a faster and more efficient way to move goods.

On the coastal regions, Mayas used large seagoing canoes. Christopher Columbus saw a Mayan canoe in 1502, during his fourth voyage to the Americas. He recorded that it was over 50 feet long and about eight feet wide and had a cabin structure and a crew of about 12 men.

The Court of a Thousand Columns was a market in Chichén Itzá.

Marketplaces

Most of the Mayan trade was directly between merchants, who then resold goods. Some villages became major trading centers. The villagers built large stone warehouses in which goods were stored. Larger Mayan cities had great marketplaces. One of the most famous markets was in the **Court of a Thousand Columns**. This was a plaza next to the Temple of the Warriors in Chichén Itzá.

The Barter System

The Mayas used the barter system. **Barter** is the exchange of certain goods for others. Money is not used in this system. The Mayas did not have money. At times, they used cacao beans instead of money. One record shows that a slave was worth 100 cacao beans.

The Mayas traded fruits and vegetables as well as salt, honey, dried fish, turtle eggs, deer meat, and birds. They also exchanged many non-food items. Popular goods included cotton cloth, animal skins, feathers, shells, gold, emeralds, jade, and other valuable stones. The Mayas also bought and sold slaves at the markets.

No other ancient American group became as involved in trade as the Mayas. It was not until modern days that trade again became as important to our culture.

Quetzal feathers were prized by the Mayas.

Name: _____ Date: _____

Knowledge Check

Matching

_____ 1. ppolm

_____ 2. caravans

_____ 3. canoe

_____ 4. Court of a
Thousand Columns

_____ 5. barter

a. groups of traders and slaves traveling together for safety

b. the exchange of certain goods for others

c. the Mayan name for merchants

d. a plaza in Chichén Itzá where a large market was set up

e. a narrow boat with both ends pointed that is usually moved by paddling

Multiple Choice

6. Who carried most of the trade goods from place to place?

   a. merchants
   b. donkeys
   c. llamas
   d. slaves

7. Who saw and described a Mayan seagoing canoe in 1502?

   a. Vasco da Gama
   b. Ferdinand Cortés
   c. Christopher Columbus
   d. Francisco Pizarro

8. What did the Mayans NOT use in their trading system?

   a. money
   b. barter
   c. cacao beans
   d. slaves

9. Which Mayan god was important to the merchants?

   a. Chac
   b. Ix Chel
   c. Ek Chaub
   d. Buluc Chabtan

Constructed Response

10. List some of the items the Mayas traded. Use details from the reading selection to help support your answer.

_____

_____

_____

_____

_____

_____

The Great Mayan Mystery

What Happened to the Mayas?

One of the great mysteries in the history of civilization is what happened to the Mayas. The Mayas suddenly abandoned their cities about A.D. 850. The Mayan society collapsed, and the people scattered through the countryside. Scholars have formed many theories about the cause of the collapse. However, not one bit of proof of any of these theories exists.

Natural Disaster

Some people believe that a natural disaster caused the Mayas to desert the cities. Perhaps an earthquake or a hurricane forced them to leave suddenly. Was an **epidemic** of a disease such as yellow fever the cause? Perhaps they had to leave so quickly that no one had time to carve stones that would tell the story.

Tikal, in northern Guatemala, was the largest Mayan city. It and the other Mayan cities were abandoned in about A.D. 850.

Agricultural Failure

Others believe that the Mayas left due to agricultural reasons. Perhaps the Mayan system of farming exhausted the soil. The crops could no longer feed the large population. The Mayas did not develop new planting methods. They always used the planting stick. They never discovered how to use a plow. This limited the size of the crops. The Mayas did not use animals nor wheeled vehicles. The only way to transport food from the fields to the cities was by **man power**. This limited how far away from the city the Mayas could plant crops. If this theory is true, the people had to leave the cities to avoid hunger.

Peasant Revolt

Another theory is that the **peasants** may have revolted against the rulers. The peasants worked very hard. Most of their labor provided food and wealth to the upper classes. Did the peasants refuse to continue their work? The upper classes would have had to leave the cities to survive if the peasants left the farms.

Outside Attack

Still other people believe that invaders attacked and conquered the cities. Perhaps other tribes such as the **Toltecs** took over the cities and forced the Mayas to leave.

The mystery of the last days of the Mayas is still being debated. We have no proof of any one of the theories. Will scientists discover something in the Mayan ruins that will give us a clue to the answer? Will we ever find the answer to the great mystery of the Mayas?

Name: _____ Date: _____

Knowledge Check

Matching

_____ 1. epidemic

_____ 2. man power

_____ 3. peasants

_____ 4. Toltecs

a. an outbreak of disease that affects a large number of people at the same time

b. people who became the most important tribe in the region after the Mayas left

c. the poor people who worked the land

d. human strength or effort without the help of machines

Fact/Opinion

Place an *F* on the line if the statement is a fact. Place an *O* on the line if it is an opinion.

_____ 5. Mayan peasants may have revolted against their rulers.

_____ 6. The Mayas never developed new farming methods, such as using plows, animals, or wheeled vehicles.

_____ 7. A hurricane could have destroyed the Mayan cities and food supply and forced them to leave suddenly.

_____ 8. Another tribe, such as the Toltecs, may have forced the Mayas to leave.

_____ 9. The Mayas suddenly abandoned their cities about A.D. 850.

_____ 10. A disease might have wiped out most of the Mayas.

Critical Thinking

11. Knowing what you do about the Mayas, which theory in the reading selection do you think is the best explanation for what happened to them? Why? Use details from the reading selection to help support your answer.

_____

_____

_____

_____

_____

_____

_____

The Mayas and the Spanish

Mayapan

After the fall of the great Mayan cities, the Mayan people continued to live in both the highlands and lowlands of their ancestors. However, they never again achieved the greatness of the earlier Mayan civilization. **Mayapan** became the new capital in the 13th century. It was the only walled city built by the Mayas. Mayapan lasted only until about 1441, when it was destroyed.

Some tribes joined the Spaniards to attack the Mayas.

Small City-States

The Mayas settled in several other small villages. They no longer had a central government. Many independent tribes formed separate **city-states**. The Mayas continued to fight amongst themselves. These civil wars, as well as epidemics, droughts, and hurricanes, continued to weaken the Mayan tribes.

The Mayas Meet Europeans

The first meeting of Mayas and Europeans occurred in 1502. During his fourth voyage, Columbus wrote of seeing native trading canoes. Other white men came through the Mayan lands during the next few years, searching for gold and slaves.

The white men brought with them diseases that were new to the native people of the Americas. **Smallpox** was the worst of these. The natives had no resistance built up against the deadly disease. The vaccine against smallpox was not developed until centuries later, and hundreds of thousands of Native Americans soon died of the disease.

The Spanish Conquer the Mayas

The death of so many Native Americans and fighting between the tribes helped the Spanish conquer the land. Hernando Cortés led several conquest groups through the Mayan lands between 1519 and 1525. Other Spanish expeditions followed. By 1542 the Spanish had built their own capital city, Mérida. Mérida is now the capital of the state of Yucatan, Mexico.

The conquest of the Mayas lasted for many years. It was a bloody and brutal defeat. The Mayas could not compete against the superior arms and **cavalry** of the enemy. Often, some Mayan tribes joined the Spanish against other tribes. The Mayan armies also lost many warriors to disease.

After a short battle, the Spanish conquered the last Mayan kingdom, **Tayasal**, in 1697. With the fall of Tayasal, the Spanish destroyed the last remnants of the once great Mayan civilization.

Name: _____ Date: _____

Knowledge Check

Matching

_____ 1. Mayapan

_____ 2. city-states

_____ 3. smallpox

_____ 4. cavalry

_____ 5. Tayasal

a. soldiers mounted on horses

b. independent units of government formed around cities

c. the last Mayan kingdom

d. the new Mayan capital in the 13th century

e. a deadly disease brought by the Europeans to which the natives had no resistance

Multiple Choice

6. What was different about the city of Mayapan?

    a. It was destroyed.

    c. It was a walled city.

    b. It was in the Yucatan Peninsula.

    d. It was built by the Mayas.

7. What were the white men from Europe searching for in the Mayan lands?

    a. food

    c. lumber

    b. gold and slaves

    d. salt and cacao

8. What was the name of the Spanish capital in this region?

    a. Tayasal

    c. Tikal

    b. Mayapan

    d. Mérida

9. Often, Mayans joined the Spanish to fight against

    a. other white men.

    c. jaguars.

    b. other Mayans.

    d. the Toltecs.

Constructed Response

10. What four things continued to weaken the Mayan civilization? Use details from the reading selection to help support your answer.

_____

_____

_____

_____

_____

_____

The Toltecs

The Toltecs Become Powerful

Small tribes of people scattered throughout the central Mexico region after the fall of the great city Teotihuacan. Wandering tribes also moved into the Valley of Mexico from the northern regions. One group soon became the most important and powerful tribe in the region. Today we call the people of this tribe **Toltecs**. Their civilization lasted from about A.D. 900 to 1200.

Topiltzin Founds Tula

The first great ruler of the Toltecs was Mixcoatl. His son, **Topiltzin**, became a legendary figure. He founded the city of **Tula**. Tula is about 60 miles north of Mexico City. Tula means "place of the reeds." It soon became the capital and largest city of the Toltecs.

Toltec legends say Topiltzin was a peaceful ruler. His god was **Quetzalcoatl**, a peaceful, feathered snake. His enemies worshipped the war-loving god **Tezcatlipoca**. Topiltzin and his followers lost to the warlords and had to leave the city.

The Temple of Quetzalcoatl in Tula was adorned with carved stone columns that supported its roof.

The Toltecs Become Fierce Warriors

With the departure of Topiltzin, the Toltecs soon became fierce warriors. They built a society ruled by the military. They demanded tributes from the people whom they conquered. Many of the captives of war became sacrifices to the gods, since the Toltecs had begun to include human sacrifices in their religious ceremonies. A sculpture of a skull rack remains in the ruins of Tula. This is a reminder of these ceremonies.

Trade With the Mayas

The Toltecs had contact with the Mayas. Trade existed between the cities of Tula and Chichén Itzá in Yucatan. Similar styles of art appear in the ruins of both cities.

Temple of Quetzalcoatl

The ruins of Tula contain several pyramids and temples. The most famous is the Temple of Quetzalcoatl, the feathered serpent god of Topiltzin and his followers. Large stone columns carved in the forms of serpents and humans supported the roof of the temple.

The Toltecs Lose Power

The Toltec citizens suffered from serious **droughts**. This weakened their military strength. Outside tribes then conquered the Toltec cities. These enemies destroyed Tula in about 1150. Many years later, the Aztecs reused parts of the buildings of Tula in their cities. The Toltecs greatly influenced the Aztecs. In addition to the Aztecs, many other tribes proudly claimed to descend from the Toltecs.

Name: _____ Date: _____

Knowledge Check

Matching

_____ 1. Toltecs

_____ 2. Topiltzin

_____ 3. Tula

_____ 4. Quetzalcoatl

_____ 5. Tezcatlipoca

_____ 6. droughts

a. a peaceful god, represented by a feathered snake

b. the capital and largest city of the Toltecs

c. long periods without rain

d. a war-loving god

e. a peaceful ruler who founded the city of Tula

f. wandering tribe that settled in central Mexico and became the most powerful tribe in the region from A.D. 900 to 1200

Multiple Choice

7. Where was the Toltec civilization located?

    a. Valley of Mexico

    c. Pacific coast of Mexico

    b. Yucatan Peninsula

    d. far northern Mexico

8. Who was the first great ruler of the Toltecs?

    a. Topiltzin

    c. Quetzalcoatl

    b. Mixcoatl

    d. Tezcatlipoca

9. After Topiltzin was forced to leave, the Toltec society was ruled by

    a. the priests.

    c. the farmers.

    b. the teachers.

    d. the military.

Constructed Response

10. How did the Toltecs treat those people they conquered? Use details from the reading selection to help support your answer.

_____

_____

_____

_____

_____

_____

_____

Name: _____ Date: _____

Explore: The City of Tula Maze

Can you find your way through the maze of the Toltec city of Tula?

START HERE

YOU MADE IT!

The Incas

The early history of the Incas is a mystery. Since the Incas never developed a system of writing, we must rely on the writings of their Spanish conquerors for any Incan history that we know. We can also study artifacts of the ancient cities for clues to the early Incas' story.

Incan Myths

We do know some Incan myths. One early story is that the sun god created the first Incan, **Manco Capac**, and his sister. The god told them to go and teach other Indians. They went into the wilderness to establish a city. They named their city **Cuzco**, and it became the capital of the Incan empire.

Manco Capac and his sister, Mama Uqllu, were the first Incas.

The Incan Territory

The Incas probably began as one of many small tribes in the **Andes Mountains**. At its peak, the Incan empire spread through parts of what are now Peru, Ecuador, Chile, Bolivia, and Argentina. The Incan land included desert, fertile valleys, some rain forests, and the Andes Mountains.

The Incas conquered most of their territory under the leadership of Pachacutec, who ruled from 1438 to 1471. The Incas crushed most of the other tribes during brutal fighting.

The Incan empire was so large that they built a system of roads that stretched over 12,000 miles. The Incas did not use wheeled vehicles on their roads. The great road system was for **pedestrians**. Only the road system of the ancient Romans was equal to that of the Incas.

The Incan Culture

The Incas developed terrace farming. They cut **terraces** into the steep sides of the mountains to create more farm land. They also dug irrigation systems to bring water from the mountain streams to the terraces. Many of the Incan roads, terraces, and irrigation ditches are still in use today.

A quipu was used for counting and keeping records.

The llama was an important animal for the Incas. They tamed the llama and used it for transportation of men and materials. The llama also provided the Incas with wool and food.

The Incas developed a counting system that used a base of ten. They used a *quipu* to remember numbers. The quipu had a main cord about two feet long. They tied many colored strings to the main cord. Each string had knots tied in it. The color of the strings and the distance between the knots had special meanings.

The Spanish Invade

The Incan civilization was at its peak when the Spanish arrived. Francisco Pizarro led the Spanish invaders against the Incas. After a series of fierce battles, the Spanish defeated the Incan king, Atahualpa, and in 1533 he was killed. The descendants of the Incas, like those of the Mayas and Aztecs, continued to live under the rule of the Spanish.

Name: _____ Date: _____

Knowledge Check

Matching

_____ 1. Manco Capac

_____ 2. Cuzco

_____ 3. Andes Mountains

_____ 4. pedestrians

_____ 5. terraces

_____ 6. quipu

a. the capital city of the Incan empire

b. a knotted and colored cord device used for counting by the Incas

c. according to myth, the first Incan created by the sun god

d. mountain range that runs along the western edge of South America; home of the Incas

e. ridges cut into the steep sides of mountains to create more level farm land

f. people who walk from place to place

Multiple Choice

7. The Incas conquered most of their territory under which leader?

    a. Manco Capac

    c. Pachacutec

    b. Atahualpa

    d. Huscar

8. What animal provided the Incas with food, wool, and a way to transport men and goods?

    a. llama

    c. camel

    b. elephant

    d. donkey

9. Who was the leader of the Spanish invaders who defeated the Incas?

    a. Hernando Cortés

    c. Vasco Nuñez de Balboa

    b. Francisco Pizarro

    c. Ponce de León

Constructed Response

10. Why is so little known about the early history of the Incas? What can we look at to find out about the Incas? Use details from the reading selection to help support your answer.

_____

_____

_____

_____

_____

_____

_____

Name: _____ Date: _____

Map Follow-Up: The Incan Empire

The Incan empire included parts of the countries that are now Peru, Ecuador, Chile, Bolivia, and Argentina.

1. Using a globe, atlas, or map, label those countries on the map below.

2. Use a colored pencil or crayon and color in these countries to show the approximate size of the Incan empire.

3. Label the locations of the following: The Caribbean Sea, the Atlantic Ocean, and the Pacific Ocean.

Incan Religion

Gods and Goddesses

Like other native tribes, the Incas worshipped many gods and goddesses. The major Incan god was the god of nature, **Viracocha**, the creator.

Another Incan god was **Inti**, the sun god. Gold was the symbol of Inti. The sun god temple is the most important structure in Cuzco, the major city of the Incas. The Incas believed Inti was the father of Incan rulers. They worshipped the ruler as a living god.

Major Incan goddesses included those of the earth and the sea. The Incas also worshipped many lesser gods and goddesses. These included gods of thunder, the moon, stars, rainbows, and others.

The Incas believed they could learn the will of the gods by divining. **Divining** is studying objects to find magic signs. Priests would look at things such as animal organs, flames of a fire, or movements of animals, and from these they would try to discover if it was a good day for planting crops, going to war, or making other important decisions.

Viracocha has a rayed head- dress and carries staffs.

Huacas

In addition to the gods and goddesses, the Incas worshipped *huacas*. A huaca was a sacred place or thing. Huacas included mummies of the dead, temples, holy places, and things of nature such as mountains, springs, and stones. Each Incan family had small statues in their homes of huacas. The statues were sacred to that family.

Religious ceremonies were an important part of Incan life. Each family had daily prayers to their huacas. The priests performed daily ceremonies at the various temples. The high priest was a favorite relative of the ruler.

The festival of Inti Raimi is held in June.

Religious Festivals

The Incas held a major religious festival during each of the 12 months of their calendar. The Incan year began in December with the **Capac Raimi**. This means "the magnificent festival." This was the most important and elaborate of all celebrations. **Pauca Huaray**, in March, celebrated the ripening of the earth. The June ceremony of **Inti Raimi** was the festival of the Sun. **Uma Raimi**, the festival of the water, occurred in October.

Some rituals happened inside the temples. The great monthly festivals occurred outdoors. All of the people could take part in them. The celebrations included dancing, feasts, games, songs, and parades. The ceremonies also included sacrifices and offerings. Incas sacrificed animals such as the llama and guinea pigs. At times human sacrifices, including child sacrifices, were part of the rituals.

Name: _____ Date: _____

Knowledge Check

Matching

_____ 1. Virachocha   a. the sun god

_____ 2. Inti   b. the god of nature; the creator

_____ 3. divining   c. a sacred place or thing

_____ 4. huaca   d. studying objects to find magic signs

Multiple Choice

5. Which of the 12 montly festivals was "the magnificent festival" that was the most important and elaborate celebration of the year?
   a. Inti Raimi
   b. Capac Raimi
   c. Pauca Huaray
   d. Uma Raimi

6. Which was the festival of the water that occurred in October?
   a. Inti Raimi
   b. Capac Raimi
   c. Pauca Huaray
   d. Uma Raimi

7. What was NOT one of the ways priests would try to determine if it was a good day to plant crops?
   a. look at the calendar
   b. look at animal organs
   c. watch the flames of a fire
   d. study the movements of animals

8. How was the Incan high priest chosen?
   a. The people voted for him.
   b. He was picked at random.
   c. He was a favorite relative of the ruler.
   d. He proved himself by predicting the future.

9. Which of the following is NOT an example of a huaca?
   a. the thunder god
   b. a mummy
   c. a temple
   c. a mountain

Constructed Response

10. Why did the Incas worship their ruler as a living god? Use details from the reading selection to help support your answer.

   _____

   _____

   _____

   _____

   _____

Name: _____ Date: _____

Explore: Incan Gods and Goddesses

Mosaics

Materials needed: large sheet of paper, pieces of colored paper, scissors, and paste.

On this page are illustrations taken from Incan temples. These are of four of the Incan gods. Using a marker or crayon, create a large drawing of one of these gods. It does not have to be an exact copy. If you would prefer, make your own drawing of a figure using the Incan style. Next, cut pieces of various colors of paper and glue them into the spaces created by your drawing. You have made a mosaic. Ancient artists used various colored stones to make their mosaics.

The eye areas of the mosaic could be cut out and string attached to the sides to make a mask to wear. Perhaps you and your classmates could make a bulletin board of the mosaics you make.

GOD OF THUNDER AND LIGHTNING

MOTHER EARTH GODDESS

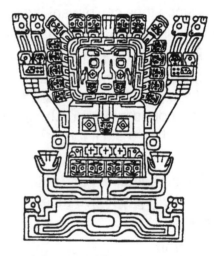

SUN GOD

MOON GODDESS

Incan Agriculture

Incan Crops

Many of the foods we use today were also part of the Incan diet. Incan farmers grew a greater variety of crops than any other ancient American tribe. They grew potatoes, corn, tomatoes, avocados, peppers, strawberries, peanuts, cashews, squash, beans, pineapples, cacao, and other crops.

Using step-like terraces carved into the mountain sides, the Incas created more flat land for crops. The terraces, which are still used today, also helped control soil erosion.

Potatoes

The potato was the most important food of the Incas. They called it **papa**. The Incas had many varieties and colors of potatoes, and today we know of 40 of those varieties. The potato became the main source of food for the Incas since they could plant it at great heights in the Andes Mountains. Some of the varieties of potato would also resist the frosts of the region.

The Incas used the first known freeze-dried process. They left the potatoes outside to freeze. Then the Incas trampled the potatoes by foot to squeeze the water out of them. Next they left them in the sunlight to dry. The Incas called these dried potatoes **chuñu**. The Incas preserved chuñu either whole or ground into flour. Chuñu would last for years without spoiling and was easy to store. The Incas were able to eat it throughout the year.

Corn

Corn was another important Incan crop. The Incas planted over 20 varieties of corn. Corn is called maize by many native tribes. However, the Incas named it **sara**. Corn was grown only in the lower regions.

Terraced Farming

The mountains presented farmers with special challenges. To create enough flat land for the crops, the Incas carved flat step-like **terraces** into the mountain sides. The terraces also helped to keep the soil from being eroded. Modern Andes farmers still use many of the ancient Incan terraces.

Planting the crops was a group effort. The men would break up the soil with planting sticks. The women then followed, putting the seeds into the earth. The children often worked in the fields to scare away birds and animals that might eat the crops before the harvest.

The Incas also developed a system to carry the water of the mountain streams to the terraces. They dug canals and tunnels and built raised **aqueducts** to carry the water. The Incan water system is still in use today.

Farming and Religion

Farming was the subject of many Incan religious ceremonies. After the planting season, the Incas made sacrifices to the rain god. At another major festival, the Incas thanked the gods for a good harvest.

Name: _____ Date: _____

Knowledge Check

Matching

_____ 1. papa

_____ 2. chuñu

_____ 3. sara

_____ 4. terraces

_____ 5. aqueducts

a. the Incan name for corn

b. ridges cut into the mountain sides to make more level land for farming

c. freeze-dried potatoes

d. the Incan name for potatoes

e. a structure for carrying flowing water, usually from a river or stream to other locations

Multiple Choice

6. What was the most important food of the Incas?

   a. chocolate

   c. squash

   b. corn

   d. potatoes

7. Who worked in the fields to scare away birds and animals so they couldn't eat the crops?

   a. women

   c. children

   b. men

   d. dogs

8. Canals, tunnels, and aqueducts were used to bring what to the terraces?

   a. water

   c. fertilizer

   b. seeds

   d. people

9. Potatoes could be grown at great heights in the

   a. Amazon jungle.

   c. coastal region.

   b. lowlands.

   d. Andes Mountains.

Constructed Response

10. What might make you believe that the Incas designed things to last? Use details from the reading selection to help support your answer.

_____

_____

_____

_____

_____

_____

Incan Weaving

Weaving was one of the most important crafts of the ancient Incas. The women did most of the dying, spinning, and weaving of cloth. However, many Incan men were also weavers.

Types of Wool

The Incas used wool for weaving most of their cloth. **Llama** wool is very coarse and is varied in color. The Incas used it to make blankets and ropes. Wool from the alpaca is white with some gray and brown. The Incas used **alpaca** wool to weave clothing. The wool from the **vicuña** is a soft fiber. They used vicuña wool for weaving the finest cloth. When the Spanish invaders first saw cloth woven from vicuña wool, they thought it was silk.

Incan methods for producing fabrics have remained unchanged for thousands of years.

Cotton

Cotton could not be grown in the mountain regions of the Incas. When the Incan empire spread to the coast, cotton became available through trade with other tribes and soon became popular with the Incan weavers.

Types of Looms

Three types of looms were used by Incan weavers. The most unusual was the **backstrap loom**. They tied one end of the loom to a tree. They then tied the other end to a belt that went around the weaver's back. The Incas also used a **horizontal loom**. It was stretched about a foot off the ground between wooden supports. They also used a **vertical loom**, attached to a wall. The weaver using this loom would stand to work.

Dyes

Incan cloth had bright, bold colors. They obtained the colors to dye the wool from many sources. They used metals such as copper and tin for some of the dyes. The Incas also used vegetable dyes. The **indigo** plant gave a bright blue dye, and the **achiote** tree was the source of a brilliant red dye. A dye made from ground **shellfish** provided a deep purple color.

Making Cloth

Several steps were necessary in the production of wool cloth. The Incas gathered the wool from the animals. The women then dyed the wool. After drying it, they spun the wool into thread. Next, they wove the thread into cloth. The Incan weavers used geometric patterns. Seldom did a weaver repeat the same pattern.

The Incas used **embroidery** to decorate some of the cloth. Some of the better garments had decorations of gold, silver, or copper attached to them, and some garments had feathers woven into them for extra color and decoration.

A group of women called the "chosen women" lived in the temples. They wove the finest wool into garments for the ruler. He only wore each garment once, and then it was destroyed.

Today, descendants of the ancient Incas still weave beautiful, bright textiles. The methods and designs used have remained unchanged for about 3,000 years.

Name: _____ Date: _____

Knowledge Check

Matching

_____ 1. cotton

_____ 2. backstrap loom

_____ 3. horizontal loom

_____ 4. vertical loom

_____ 5. indigo

_____ 6. achiote

_____ 7. embroidery

a. attached to a wall; the weaver would stand to use it

b. a plant that was used for blue dye

c. a plant whose fibers can be spun into thread

d. tied to a tree and a belt that went around the weaver's back

e. fancy stitching sewn on cloth

f. a tree that was used for brilliant red dye

g. stretched about a foot off the ground between wooden supports

Multiple Choice

8. Which material was used to make the finest cloth?

   a. llama wool

   b. cotton

   c. vicuña wool

   d. alpaca wool

9. Which item produced a deep purple colored dye?

   a. achiote tree

   b. ground shellfish

   c. indigo plant

   d. copper

10. Who wove the finest wool into garments for the Incan ruler?

   a. the chosen women

   b. the palace weavers

   c. the royal loomers

   d. the high priests

Constructed Response

11. Explain the steps in the production of wool cloth. Use details from the reading selection to help support your answer.

_____

_____

_____

_____

_____

_____

_____

_____

Incan Arts and Crafts

Metalwork

The Incas are most famous for their weaving, but they also developed skills in metalwork. They used gold, silver, copper, and tin. They discovered how to make **bronze** by melting copper and tin together. Incan men mined the precious metals. They did not use slaves to work in the mines. Instead, the Incas did this work as part of their "**work tax**." The Incas had to give a certain amount of their labor to the government.

All of the gold became the property of the ruler. Metal workers pounded much of the gold into thin sheets to cover the walls of the palaces. They also made statues and other decorations for the ruler. The ruler and nobles also used silver for decoration.

Incans were known for their metalwork.

They believed that silver was the metal of the moon. Craftsmen also used gold and silver to make masks, plates, and jewelry.

Spanish invaders reported seeing life-size statues made of bronze and covered in gold. After the conquests of the Incas, the Spaniards melted down most of the Incan gold and shipped it to Spain. Very few Incan artworks made of gold still exist.

Copper, tin, and bronze were also used to make artistic, as well as useful, items. Archeologists have found many examples of Incan metal items such as knives, weapons, pins for garments, and tools.

Pottery

Only small Incan statues remain. The Spaniards melted down everything else.

The Incas also created a variety of pottery. Examples survive of three-legged pots, plates, and drinking cups. One of the most well-known examples of Incan pottery was the **aryballus**. This was a jar with a cone-shaped bottom. It was used to store liquids. Much of Incan pottery had knobs attached to it to which ropes could be tied for carrying.

The Incas made most of their pottery for use rather than art. Even so, it was beautiful. Their pottery is known for its elaborate yet small **geometric** patterns.

The Incas also had a special method of applying colors to the pottery. However, the secret of the ancient Incan method of coloring pottery is lost. Most Incan pottery was red, white, and black. At times, they also used yellow and orange.

The crafts of weaving, metalwork, and pottery are still being done by the descendants of the ancient Incas. They still use many of the same methods and designs of their ancestors.

Even though Incan pottery was made for practical use, pieces were highly decorated.

Name: _____ Date: _____

Knowledge Check

Matching

_____ 1. bronze

_____ 2. work tax

_____ 3. aryballus

_____ 4. geometric

a. a jar with a cone-shaped bottom that was used to store liquids

b. the requirement that all Incas had to give a certain amount of their labor to the government

c. designs based on simple shapes, such as straight lines, circles, or squares

d. metal made by melting copper and tin together

True/False

Place a *T* on the blank if the statement is true or an *F* if it is false.

_____ 5. The Incas made life-size statues of bronze covered in gold.

_____ 6. Slaves were used to mine gold and other precious metals.

_____ 7. People today still color pottery the same way the ancient Incas did.

_____ 8. All the gold became the property of the Incan ruler.

_____ 9. There are many pieces of Incan artwork made of gold still around today.

_____ 10. The Incas believed that silver was the metal of the moon.

Constructed Response

11. What were some of the practical items for everyday use the Incas made out of metal and pottery? Use details from the reading selection to help support your answer.

_____

_____

_____

_____

_____

_____

_____

_____

Incan Roads and Bridges

The Incan Transportation System

The Incas built one of the ancient world's best transportation systems. They built roads and bridges to keep the empire together. The transportation system allowed them to have fast communication between villages and cities. They also used it to move food and other supplies. The roads also allowed military troops to move faster.

Incan Roads

The Incan roads stretched for more than 10,000 miles. The Incas had two major roads. The **Royal Road** was 3,250 miles long. It went from the northern border of the empire through Ecuador, Peru, and Bolivia into Argentina and Chile.

The other major road, the **coastal highway**, was 2,520 miles long. It ran from the village of Tumbes in the north, through the desert, then into Chile.

This hanging rope bridge is renewed every year with traditional methods once used by the Incas.

Several other roads ran between the two major ones. The standard width of the roads was 24 feet. They were narrower only when natural barriers were in the way. The roads included side walls to keep out sand drifts and to mark the road. There were also markers along the road to tell the distance to the next village.

Incan workers provided the labor to build the roads as part of the "**labor tax**" they paid to the government. Government engineers directed the workers.

The roads belonged to the government. No one could use the road without special permission. The Incas did not use wheeled vehicles on their roads. The travelers and messengers walked to their destinations. The Incas used llamas to carry goods on the roads. They built rest houses called *tampus* about every 12 to 20 miles along the roads. In addition to providing a place to rest, most tampus also had food available.

Incan Bridges

The Incas built causeways to elevate the roads in swampy areas. They also built amazing bridges, which they called *chacas*. The hanging bridges are the most famous of the Incan chacas. One Incan bridge was over 250 feet long. Built in 1350, it lasted until 1890.

The Incas used the fibers of the **maguey plant** to weave the cable for the bridges. The main cables were from four to five feet thick. Incan workers had to replace the cables about every two years.

The Incas also built pontoon bridges made of reed boats tied together. Another type of Incan bridge had a basket hung from a cable stretched between two stone towers. Travelers got into the basket, and a workman then pulled along the cable to the other side.

Name: _____ Date: _____

Knowledge Check

Matching

_____ 1. labor tax

_____ 2. coastal highway

_____ 3. maguey

_____ 4. Royal Road

_____ 5. tampus

_____ 6. chacas

a. Stretched from the northern border through Ecuador, Peru, Bolivia, and into Argentina and Chile

b. Stretched from the village of Tumbes through the desert and into Chile

c. fibers from this plant were used to weave the cable for Incan bridges

d. what the Incas called their bridges

e. workers built the roads to pay this to the Incan government

f. rest houses along the Incan roads

Multiple Choice

7. What material was used to make the boats for pontoon bridges?

   a. maguey fibers
   c. oak

   b. reeds
   d. stone

8. How wide were most Incan roads?

   a. 6 feet
   c. 18 feet

   b. 10 feet
   d. 24 feet

9. What did the Incas use to carry their goods on the roads?

   a. sleds
   c. llamas

   b. wheeled carts
   d. horses

Constructed Response

10. Why would rope bridges have to be repaired or replaced every year or so? Use what you know about rope and details from the reading selection to support your answer.

   _____

   _____

   _____

   _____

   _____

Cities of the Incas

Well-Planned Cities

The Incas were master builders. They had the best planned cities in the ancient Americas. Planners laid out the cities in a grid. Each city had a central **plaza**, with the major temples and public buildings surrounding it. The center of each city included temples, a palace for the visiting Inca, and housing for the priests and nobles. Houses for the common people surrounded the central area.

Protection

A wall that was 50 feet high encircled the city of Chimu. However, most Incan cities did not have walls around them. The Incas built large stone **fortresses** near the city. The citizens would gather inside the fortress in time of danger.

Incan architects used trapezoidal openings for the doors and windows in their buildings.

The Santo Domingo church in Cuzco was built on the remains of the Inti-Huasi temple because the Incan stone foundation was so solidly built.

Building Methods

Incan buildings remain among the most amazing ever built. The Incas used huge blocks of stone. One stone measured 36 x 18 x 6 feet. They cut and polished each stone with small stone tools and then moved each stone into the proper place. The stones fit together perfectly, so the builders did not need to use cement to keep them in place. Even today, a knife blade cannot fit into the cracks between the stones of the ancient buildings.

The Incas used **trapezoidal** openings for all of their doors and windows. The four-sided openings were smaller at the top than at the bottom. The Incas did not decorate the outside of their buildings, but they made beautiful decorations for the insides of the palaces and temples. They often used solid gold for these decorations.

Cuzco

The two most famous Incan cities are Cuzco and Machu Picchu. Incan legend says that the first Incan ruler founded Cuzco. This happened in about A.D. 1100. **Cuzco** soon became capital of the entire empire. It is in a mountain valley about 11,000 feet above sea level. Two rivers flowed into the valley to supply water. Wars and invaders destroyed the ancient city. In 1400 Cuzco was rebuilt. The new city had two large plazas, the Inca's palace, the Sun Temple, and other temples and government buildings.

Machu Picchu

The best preserved Incan city is **Machu Picchu**. Explorers rediscovered it in 1911. Its ruins include temples, palaces, military buildings, and common houses. The Incas of Machu Picchu built terraces for farming. They also had a stone aqueduct to bring in water from a mile away.

Machu Piccu was rediscovered in 1911

50

Name: _____ Date: _____

Knowledge Check

Matching

_____ 1. plaza

_____ 2. fortress

_____ 3. trapezoid

_____ 4. Cuzco

_____ 5. Machu Picchu

a. a large structure built of stone where citizens would gather in times of danger

b. the best preserved Incan city; rediscovered in 1911

c. a large open area surrounded by public buildings

d. the capital of the Incan empire

e. four-sided shape with the top smaller than the bottom

Multiple Choice

6. Where did the Incas decorate their temples and palaces?

   a. on the outside

   b. on the inside

   c. on the roofs

   d. They did not decorate.

7. There was a palace in each Incan city. Who stayed there?

   a. the mayor of the city

   b. the priests

   c. the ruling Inca when he visited

   d. the soldiers of the Incan army

8. Where did Machu Picchu get its water?

   a. from two rivers in the valley

   b. from a deep well

   c. from rainwater collected in tanks

   d. from a source a mile away through a stone aqueduct

9. Which Incan city was surrounded by a wall?

   a. Cuzco

   b. Machu Picchu

   c. Chimu

   d. Cajamarca

Constructed Response

10. Describe how the Incas constructed their buildings. Use details from the reading selection to help support your answer.

_____

_____

_____

_____

_____

_____

_____

The Inca and His Government

The Inca

Inca was the title of the ruler of the Incan empire. At first, the word **Inca** meant "the children of the sun god Inti." It later became the title of the ruler. Today, we also use Inca to mean the people of this civilization.

The ancient Incas believed their ruler was a descendant of the gods. They worshiped him as both a god and a ruler, and he had absolute power.

The Inca was carried in a golden litter by servants.

The Inca's Family

The Inca had many wives. His main wife was his queen. Her title was **coya**. The Inca's sister could also be his coya. The Inca might have over 100 children. The oldest son of the Inca did not automatically become the next ruler; instead, a council of nobles chose the next ruler. Usually, the council chose the most promising son of the coya. At times the selection of the new Inca led to fighting among the supporters of various sons.

The Inca's Lifestyle

A **borla**, or Incan crown, was worn by the Inca. It had a fringe of brightly colored cords. Gold tubes decorated the end of each cord. The Inca wore garments of the finest wool. Each of his garments was worn only once. The Inca ate and drank only from gold plates and goblets. Servants carried the Inca on a platform and chair made of gold since he didn't walk great distances. The chair, called a **litter**, had a canopy of gold and jewels to protect the Inca from rain and the rays of the sun. Each Inca had a new palace built. The walls of the Inca's palace were decorated with gold. The Inca's throne was also gold.

The empire had a 30-day period of mourning after the death of the Inca. Priests mummified the Inca's body. Many of the Inca's servants volunteered to die, because they believed that they would then be able to continue to serve the Inca. The old palace became a shrine for the previous Inca. They put the Inca's mummified body into the shrine, and the people then worshiped the mummies of the Incas.

The Government

The Incas had an efficient government. The rulers, priests, and generals all came from the noble class. Most were relatives of the Inca. The Inca used the road and bridge system to help him govern. Messengers and soldiers were able to move quickly throughout the empire.

All Incan men gave the government physical labor. This was the **mita**, the work or labor tax. The government built the great palaces, public buildings, and roads with this labor.

Name: _____ Date: _____

Knowledge Check

Matching

_____ 1. Inca
_____ 2. coya
_____ 3. borla
_____ 4. litter
_____ 5. mita

a. word meaning "the children of the sun god Inti," the ruler of the Incan empire, and the people of this civilization

b. a canopy-covered chair on a platform on which the Inca was carried

c. the Incan crown

d. the main wife of the Inca or the Inca's sister

e. the work or labor tax all Incas had to pay to the government

Multiple Choice

6. The ancient Incas believed their ruler had descended from whom or what?
   a. the gods
   c. the earth
   b. the stars
   d. the spirit of the llama

7. Who chose the next ruler after the Inca died?
   a. the coya
   c. a council of nobles
   b. The people voted.
   d. There was a contest of strength.

8. What happened to the Inca when he died?
   a. His body was thrown into a volcano.
   c. His body was buried under the temple.
   b. His body was mummified.
   d. His body was burned.

9. How was the Incan government able to get the great palaces, public buildings, and roads built?
   a. They used slaves.
   c. They used the army.
   b. They paid workers to do it.
   d. They used citizens paying their work tax.

Constructed Response

10. Give some evidence that the Incan people treated the Inca like a god. Use details from the reading selection to help support your answer.

_____

_____

_____

_____

_____

_____

_____

The Incas and the Spanish Conquest

The Incas had little contact with the Mayas or the Aztecs. They did not know of the earliest arrival of the white man, nor did they know of the **Spanish conquest** of the other civilizations.

Incan Civil War

The Incan ruler, Huyayna Capac, died in 1525. He did not choose an heir to become the new ruler. Two of his sons, **Atahualpa** and **Huscar**, fought each other for this honor. Their fighting caused a bloody civil war that lasted for over five years. Atahualpa won the war and became the next ruler. He then ordered the death of thousands of Huscar's soldiers and his family.

The Spanish Arrive

The Incas soon received reports of strange-looking pale men with beards. An

After agreeing to meet with the Spanish, Atahualpa was ambushed by Pizarro and his men. Atahualpa paid a huge ransom in gold and silver, but the Spanish executed him anyway.

enemy tribe of the Incas captured a shipwrecked European on the coast of Brazil. He joined the enemies in some fighting against the Incas. He was the first white man whom the Incas ever saw. The Incas also heard stories of white men arriving in giant boats.

The first Spanish soldiers in the Incan territory landed on the Caribbean coast on May 13, 1532. Over 180 soldiers arrived to search for gold. Led by **Francisco Pizarro**, they brought with them guns, armor, a cannon, and horses. The Spanish were the first to bring horses to the new world. These strange new animals fascinated and frightened the Incas.

Atahualpa and Pizarro agreed to meet in a courtyard in the town of Cajamarca. Atahualpa and his men arrived without weapons. The Incas believed the Spanish might be gods, and so they did not want to offend the Spanish by being armed.

The Spanich Defeat the Incas

The Spanish, however, had planned an ambush. Atahualpa arrived in the courtyard carried on a gold throne. The Spanish then opened fire. They soon killed over 2,000 Incas. The Spanish captured Atahualpa and put him in a prison. Atahualpa agreed to pay the Spanish a **ransom** of enough gold and silver to fill his prison cell.

Even after he paid the ransom, the Spanish refused to free Atahualpa. They condemned Atahualpa to death and gave him a choice: would he prefer that they strangle him or burn him at the stake? He chose strangulation. With Atahualpa's death, the great Incan empire came under Spanish rule and influence.

 54

Name: _____ Date: _____

Knowledge Check

Matching

_____ 1. Spanish conquest

_____ 2. Atahualpa

_____ 3. Huscar

_____ 4. Francisco Pizarro

_____ 5. ransom

a. leader of the Spanish soldiers who conquered the Incas

b. brother who lost the Incan civil war

c. the defeat of the natives of the new world by Spain

d. a payment given in exchange for the release of someone held captive

e. brother who won the Incan civil war and became the Inca; he was later executed by the Spanish

Multiple Choice

6. Who had already been defeated by the Spanish by the time the Incas saw their first Spanish soldiers?

   a. the Olmecs

   c. the Aztecs

   b. the Cherokee

   d. the Toltecs

7. What event just before the Spanish arrived had weakened the Incan army?

   a. an outbreak of disease

   c. a hurricane

   b. a civil war

   d. a food shortage

8. The Incas thought the Spanish might be what?

   a. gods

   c. aliens

   b. devils

   d. friendly

9. What animal appeared in the new world for the first time thanks to the Spanish?

   a. snake

   c. alpaca

   b. horse

   d. jaguar

Critical Thinking

10. Why was the ransom of gold and silver not enough to satisfy the Spanish? Use details from the reading selection to help support your answer.

_____

_____

_____

_____

_____

_____

The Aztecs

The Aztec capital, Tenochtitlan, was built on an island in Lake Texcoco.

Tenochtitlan

The Aztec Indians had already built one of the most advanced civilizations in the western hemisphere by the time Columbus made his first voyage to the Americas. Archeologists believe that the Aztec capital **Tenochtitlan** may have had a population of over 200,000. This was larger than any city in Spain or England during the same time.

Mythology tells that the Aztecs began as wandering tribes in the north or northwest part of Mexico. This territory, called **Aztlan**, is the source of the name Aztec. Today we refer to the people as Aztecs, but they called themselves Mexica or Tenochca.

The ancient tribes wandered for many years. In the 1200s, they began to settle in the **Valley of Mexico**, which is in the central part of the country. The area rises about 7,500 feet above sea level. It is surrounded by tropical rain forests, but the high altitude gave the region a mild climate.

Nahuatl was the language spoken by the Aztecs. Many words we use today came from this ancient language. Aztec words include Acapulco, Mexico, avocado, chocolate, and tomato. The Aztecs developed a form of picture writing. Some pictures represented ideas; other pictures stood for sounds. They did not develop an alphabet, so their writing was limited in what it could express.

The Aztecs soon founded their greatest city, Tenochtitlan, on an island in Lake Texcoco. Eventually, that lake was filled in and became the site of Mexico City, the modern capital of Mexico.

The Aztec Empire

By the early 1400s, the Aztecs had gained control of their region and established a number of city-states. Each **city-state** had its own government and distinct culture. The three major city-states—Tenochtitlan, Texcoco, and Tlacopan—formed an alliance that became the Aztec empire. At one time, 489 cities paid tribute and taxes to the empire.

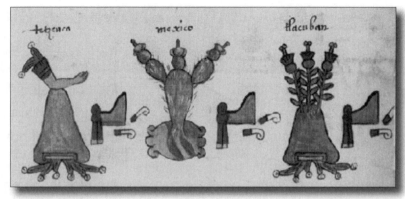

The pictorial symbols for Texcoco, Tenochtitlan, and Tlacopan.

A council of nobles always chose the emperor from members of the royal family. The greatest emperor, **Montezuma I**, ruled from 1440 to 1468/9. His name is also spelled Moctezuma and Motecuhzoma. He expanded the empire from the Atlantic to Pacific coasts and from Central America to what is now Guatemala. His grandson, Montezuma II, became emperor in 1502. He ruled when the empire was at its peak.

The Aztecs made no attempt to unify the area they commanded or to change the customs of the conquered peoples. The emperor stationed military units throughout the empire to maintain control. A great noble commanded each army and also served as governor. Most offices were hereditary, but service to the emperor was also a way to obtain a high office.

Aztec Society

Aztecs belonged to a large family group called a *calpolli*, a word that meant "big house." Each calpolli owned a plot of land to meet the needs of its members. In addition to providing necessities for their own members, each calpolli presented the government with part of the harvest as a tribute.

There were four main social classes in Aztec society. The upper-class nobles owned land in addition to the land of their calpolli. The commoners farmed the calpolli land or made crafts and gave tributes to the nobles in return for protection. Serfs who farmed the land of the nobles formed the third major class. Slaves were the lowest class. They had either been captives in war, criminals, or citizens who became unable to pay their debts. Slaves became household servants or worked alongside the serfs in the fields.

The Spanish Invasion

Spaniards, under the leadership of Hernando Cortés, invaded Mexico in search of gold. Many of the smaller city-states helped the Spanish destroy the Aztec empire in 1521. They helped the Spanish because they resented paying tributes to the Aztec empire.

The glory of the Aztec empire vanished during the Spanish invasion, but today Aztec designs still have a strong influence on Mexican art, and thousands of modern Mexicans can trace their ancestry to the Aztecs.

Name: _____ Date: _____

Knowledge Check

Matching

_____ 1. Tenochtitlan

_____ 2. Aztlan

_____ 3. Valley of Mexico

_____ 4. Nahuatl

_____ 5. city-state

_____ 6. Montezuma I

_____ 7. calpolli

a. the language spoken by the Aztecs

b. an independent government unit centered on a city

c. the region of north or northwest Mexico from which the Aztecs came

d. the region in central Mexico where the Aztecs settled

e. an Aztec family group; meant "big house"

f. the Aztec capital city

g. the greatest Aztec emperor

Multiple Choice

8. What was once at the site of Tenochtitlan and the modern-day Mexico City?

    a. a lake

    c. a desert

    b. a volcano

    d. a mountain

9. Which word below is not from the Nahuatl language?

    a. avocado

    c. Mexico

    b. chocolate

    d. quipu

10. Which social class was made up of captives in war, criminals, or citizens who couldn't pay their debts?

    a. serfs

    c. nobles

    b. slaves

    d. commoners

Constructed Response

11. How was the Aztec empire organized? Use details from the reading selection to help support your answer.

_____

_____

_____

_____

_____

_____

_____

_____

Name: _____ Date: _____

Map Follow-Up: The Aztec Empire

Using a map or atlas to help you, write the name of the following places in the proper locations on the map.

Baja California
Balsas River
Gulf of Mexico
Mexico City (This was the location of the ancient Aztec city of Tenochtitlan)
Pacific Ocean
Rio Grande
Sierra Madre Mountains
Yucatan Peninsula

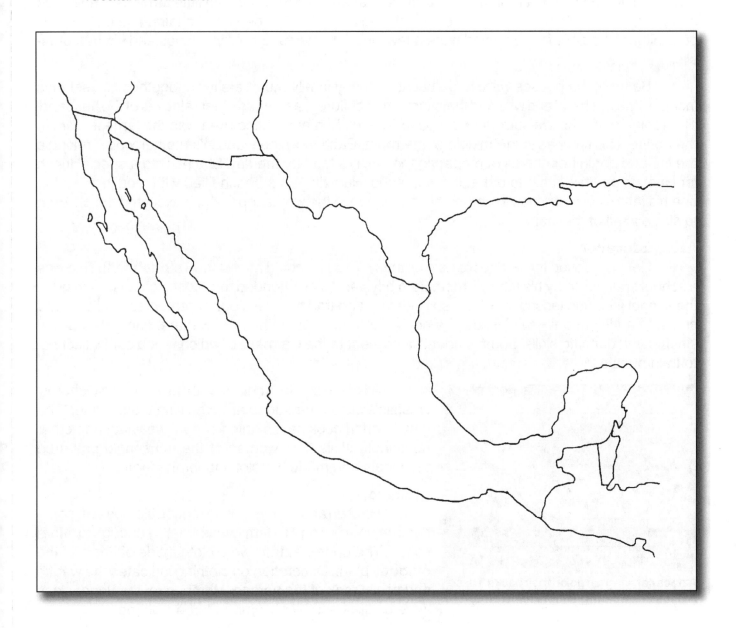

Aztec Daily Life

Huetzin woke up an hour before the sun appeared. He rolled his sleeping mat into a small bundle and put it into the corner of the room. He was still sleepy as he went into the small steam bath attached to his house. He threw some water onto the hot rocks to make the steam. As the steam subsided, he went outside and dove into the canal that ran along beside the house. He shivered at the cold water of the canal. Now he was fully awake.

Aztecs ate corn pancakes, which the Spanish called *tortillas*, twice a day.

Aztec Houses

A small house made of **adobe** brick was home to Huetzin. The house had a roof made of **thatched** straw. Aztec homes had little furniture. They used woven straw mats that were placed on the dirt floors instead of beds and chairs. The only pieces of furniture Huetzin's family owned were a few wooden chests to hold valuables and kitchen utensils.

Some of the houses were large because many family members lived together. Households included the husband and wife and their unmarried children, as well as other relatives of the husband. The rooms of the house surrounded a patio. The kitchen and eating area was the largest room in the house. The fire was in the middle of the room. Each morning Huetzin's mother would rekindle the fire and begin her chores of preparing the family's food for the day. She packed a special lunch for Huetzin and his father to eat at the workshop. Huetzin had a pouch filled with food just like the one his father carried. Huetzin carried his own lunch to the workshop. Aztecs expected the children to share in all of the work.

Aztec Education

Huetzin looked forward to his next birthday. Then he could attend the **Telpuchcalli**. This was a school sponsored by his family's tribe. Both boys and girls attended the Aztec schools. Training at the school included lessons in citizenship, history and tradition, religious ceremonies, and arts and crafts. In addition to these classes, the boys learned about methods of warfare. The girls learned singing and dancing skills. Some students also went to the **Calmecac**, which was a special school to train priests.

Aztecs carrying cargo on their backs. These Aztecs are wearing simple loincloths.

All of the children helped with the household chores. Huetzin's sisters remained at home with their mother. The girls learned cooking, spinning cotton, weaving, and other household skills. The women of the household prepared the meals and made the clothing for the family.

Clothing

Huetzin and his family wore cotton clothes with some decoration sewn on. His family was wealthy enough to afford cotton. The poorer Aztecs wore cloth made of fibers of the **maguey** plant. Decoration on clothing indicated the wealth and social rank of the person. Members of the upper class wore colorful and highly embroidered clothing.

Men wore a loincloth wrapped around their hips. Some men also wore cloaks tied over one shoulder. Aztec women wore loose, sleeveless blouses and wraparound skirts. People went barefoot most of the time, but some wore sandals made of leather or woven maguey fibers.

Learning a Craft

Most of Huetzin's relatives were farmers in the nearby fields, but his father was a craftsman. His father carved jade and other precious stones into small decorations. Every day Huetzin would go to the workshop with his father. His father taught him many things. He learned how to hunt and fish as well as how to use the tools to create beautiful objects to be sold in the market. He also learned the stories of his ancestors from his father.

Aztecs trading for quetzal feathers.

All day, Huetzin helped his father at the workshop. He looked forward to the time when he would be a master stone carver and work alongside his father. He and his father ate lunch with the others at the workshop. That afternoon Huetzin went to the marketplace and helped sell the carvings that had been made during the week.

Food

Huetzin and his father returned home just before sunset. They washed in the canal and then joined the rest of the family for supper. The women served the meal to the men of the household and then ate their own meals separately.

The Aztecs had a variety of food available. Members of the family brought **maize** (corn), beans, squash, chili peppers, and tomatoes from the fields. The men hunted to provide deer, rabbits, ducks, and geese. The Aztecs raised dogs and turkeys for additional meat. Corn was the main part of the Aztec diet. Twice daily, the women baked the cornmeal pancake, which the Spanish later called a **tortilla**. The Aztecs filled the tortillas with other foods much like our tamales and tacos today. The Aztecs did not have cattle or pigs, so they had little fat in their diets. The food was baked or boiled. Since they used many peppers in their cooking, the food was often spicy and hot.

Two special treats at the end of the meal might include chicle-zapoil or chocolate. **Chicle** came from a gum tree and is the basis for modern-day chewing gum. Chocolate was processed from the cacao bean. It was a delicacy and not served often. Many times the Aztecs flavored their chocolate with vanilla and other spices.

Family Time

After the meal, all members of the family worked on various chores. Huetzin's father mended tools for tomorrow's work. His uncle repaired a broken planting stick. The women continued working at their looms. This was Huetzin's favorite part of the day. As they worked in the dim glow of the fire, Huetzin listened to his grandfather tell stories of battles of the old days. Grandfather seemed to like the old days. Huetzin knew many of the stories by heart, but he enjoyed hearing his grandfather tell them again.

Soon it was time for Huetzin to go to bed. He went to his room and unrolled his sleeping mat. He was tired from his busy day, and it was not long before he fell asleep.

Name: _____ Date: _____

Knowledge Check

Matching

_____ 1. adobe

_____ 2. thatched

_____ 3. Telpuchcalli

_____ 4. Calmecac

_____ 5. maguey

_____ 6. chicle

a. covered with plant material, such as straw

b. a school for training Aztec priests

c. comes from the gum tree and is used in chewing gum

d. a brick made of sun-dried earth and straw

e. an Aztec school sponsored by a family calpolli

f. plant with tough fibers used in clothing for poorer Aztecs

Multiple Choice

7. What did the Aztecs have little of in their diets?
   - a. spice
   - b. sweets
   - c. vegetables
   - d. fat

8. Cornmeal pancakes were later called what by the Spanish?
   - a. tortillas
   - b. maize
   - c. flapjacks
   - d. tacos

9. What did the Aztecs sit or sleep on in their houses?
   - a. chairs
   - b. benches
   - c. cushions
   - d. woven mats

10. Who would usually not be living in an Aztec house?
    - a. unmarried children
    - b. husband and wife
    - c. a wife's brother
    - d. a husband's sister

Constructed Response

11. How would a young Aztec boy learn a craft? Use details from the reading selection to help support your answer.

   _____

   _____

   _____

   _____

   _____

   _____

   _____

Aztec Society

The Aztec Clan

The clan was the basis of all Aztec society and government. Each person was a member of an extended family. The extended family included grandparents, aunts, and uncles, as well as parents, brothers, and sisters. Groups of the extended families joined to form **clans**. Twenty clans combined to form a **tribe**.

Calpolli was the Aztec word for a clan. Calpolli came from the Aztec word calli, which meant "big house." Although some nobles owned their own land, the calpolli owned most of the land. The clan divided its land among the families.

An Aztec calpolli governed many aspects of its members' lives, including schooling and marriages.

Each calpolli elected its own officers to run its business. The calpolli was a true democracy. Most of the important decisions were made by popular vote. Aztec women did not have the right to vote, however.

Aztec Tribes

Aztec tribes met together often to take care of common needs. Each tribe chose a leader to be in the **council**. The members of the council then chose one of the leaders to be its chief. The chief was in charge of civil and religious affairs. The council enforced the laws of the clan. They also punished wrongdoers.

The council elected a second chief to be in charge of war matters. The calpolli expected all of its able-bodied men to fight in any wars. The men considered it an honor in addition to a duty to fight for their clan.

Life in the Calpolli

All aspects of its members' lives were governed by the calpolli. At the birth of a child, the parents consulted the calpolli's priest. The priest looked in the book of fate to see if the birth date was lucky. Four days later, the family held a feast to celebrate the birth and give the child a name. During the celebrations, family members showed weapons and tools to baby boys. They showed weaving items and musical instruments to the baby girls.

The Aztecs taught the children in their homes. They taught the boys methods of hunting and fishing or crafts. The women taught the girls spinning, weaving, cooking, and other household duties. At about the age of 13, the children went to schools operated by their clans. There, the boys learned about weapons and methods of war and the girls learned additional homemaking skills as well as music and dance.

The family arranged for all marriages. The boy and girl involved usually gave their consent to be married. A young person could only marry someone outside the clan. During the wedding ceremonies, the priest tied the cloaks of the bride and groom together. This was a symbol of the joining together of the two. The bride then became a member of her husband's clan.

Name: _____ Date: _____

Knowledge Check

Matching

_____ 1. clan
_____ 2. tribe
_____ 3. calpolli
_____ 4. council

a. the Aztec word for clan; meant "big house"
b. a group made up of 20 clans
c. a group with members from each tribe who chose a chief, enforced the laws, and punished wrongdoers
d. a group of extended families

True/False

Place a *T* on the line if the statement is true or an *F* if it is false.

_____ 5. All able-bodied men were expected to fight in any wars.
_____ 6. The council's second chief was in charge of religious affairs.
_____ 7. The calpolli owned most of the land.
_____ 8. Baby boys were shown weapons and tools, while girls were shown weaving items and musical instruments.
_____ 9. Young Aztecs could marry anyone they fell in love with.
_____ 10. At the age of 9, children went to schools operated by their clans.
_____ 11. Most important decisions were made by popular decision, but Aztec women did not have the right to vote.

Constructed Response

12. What were some advantages of joining together to form clans and tribes? Use details from the reading selection to help support your answer.

_____

_____

_____

_____

_____

_____

_____

_____

_____

Aztec Religion

Gods and Goddesses Rule the Days

The Aztecs worshipped many gods and goddesses. Each village and each occupation had its own patron god. A different god also watched over each day and each division of the day. The people worshipped the various gods and goddesses to attract the good forces of nature and to repel harmful powers. Each month of the calendar had a festival with music, dancing, processions, and sacrifices.

Tlazolteotl was the earth mother goddess.

The Festival of Ochpaniztli

Just before the sun rose, distant sounds of the temple drums woke young Xochitl. She dressed quickly, and as she went into the main room of the house, she saw that the rest of the family was already awake and making preparations to go to the temple for the festival of **Ochpaniztli**, the festival of the eleventh month. This celebration honored **Tlazolteotl**, the earth mother goddess. Her mother gave her a basket of corn to place on the temple altar as a tribute to the goddess Tlazolteotl.

Hundreds of people had arrived and were lining the road leading to the temple. The crowd quieted down as the beat of the drums stopped. Though they were too far away from the temple to hear what was said, Xochitl knew that the priests were now presenting the sacred chants. The chants provided magic to avoid rains at harvest and to celebrate the refreshment of Earth Mother Tlazolteotl. Xochitl knew that the next part of the ceremony would be a human sacrifice to appease the gods.

In this ceremony, a young woman impersonating the goddess of ripe corn would be the sacrifice. This was one of the few Aztec ceremonies that sacrificed a young woman. Usually the victims of the sacrifices were men who were either captives of wars or slaves. Many of the Aztec religious festivals included human sacrifices. The priest cut open the victim's chest and tore out the heart. He then placed the victim's heart on the altar of the god or goddess. In one ceremony to the god Tlaloc, sacrifices even included children. Xochitl's mother had explained the Aztec belief that the blood given in sacrifice gave the gods new strength and energy.

When Xochitl heard the drums and other music begin, she knew it was time for the **grand procession**. First came the young men of each clan, dressed in their finest ceremonial outfits. Xochitl enjoyed the colorful display of brightly painted clothing and fancy feather work that decorated the clothes. Each clan member also carried a military weapon and shield decorated with the insignia of the clan.

Xochitl watched closely until she recognized her clan's group. Pride filled Xochitl's heart as they passed. She especially enjoyed seeing her uncles and cousins in the procession. She knew that when he was older, her brother would also march with them.

After the last clan passed, groups of warriors with special rank and privileges passed by. Two of the special groups, the **Knights of the Eagle** and the **Knights of the Jaguar**, wore animal skins to represent their mascot. These two groups then staged a mock battle to entertain the crowd.

The rest of the festival day was spent visiting friends and feasting. Occasionally other special events provided entertainment and excitement. Other contests and games filled the afternoon. The most important of the games was **tlachti**. This was a fast-moving game using a rubber ball. Each team tried to score points by putting the ball through rings on the sides of the playing field.

Huitzilopochtli was the Aztec Sun god and god of war. He was also the chief god of Tenochtitlan.

The festival was over by sunset. Xochitl and her family returned home. After the evening meal, Xochitl went to bed early. She had had a busy and tiring day, but in 20 days she would be ready to celebrate the next festival.

AZTEC GODS AND GODDESSES

The ancient Aztecs worshipped over 60 gods and goddesses. This is a list of the more important ones.

NAME	DESCRIPTION
TEZCATLIPOCA	Sun god; most powerful of all gods; chief god of the town of Texcoco
HUITZILOPOCHTLI	Sun god and god of war; chief god of the town of Tenochtitlan
TLAZOLTEOTL	Mother of gods; earth goddess
TLALOC	Rain god; most important to the farmers
QUETZALCOATL	God of learning and the priesthood, also god of arts and crafts
CHICOMECOATL	Goddess of crops
CENETEOTL	God of corn
XIPE TOTEC	God of spring, planting, and re-growth
TONATIUH	A Sun god
MICTLANTECUHLI	God of the dead
XIUHTECUHTLI	Ancient fire god
CHALCHIHUITLICUE	Our Lady of the Turquoise skirt; goddess of lakes and rivers

Name: _____ Date: _____

Knowledge Check

Matching

_____ 1. Ochpaniztli

_____ 2. Tlazolteotl

_____ 3. grand procession

_____ 4. Knights of the Jaguar

_____ 5. tlachti

a. group of Aztec warriors with special rank and privileges; wore animal skins to represent their mascot

b. a fast-moving game with a rubber ball

c. the Aztec earth mother goddess

d. a parade of young men from each clan and special warrior groups

e. the festival of the eleventh month to honor Tlazolteotl

Multiple Choice

6. The young woman being sacrificed represented what?
   a. the goddess of water
   b. the goddess of ripe corn
   c. the earth mother goddess
   d. the goddess of the sky

7. What would the Knights of the Eagle and the Knights of the Jaguar do to entertain the crowd?
   a. stage a mock battle
   b. sacrifice two of their members
   c. stage a harvest ceremony
   d. compete in a tug-of-war contest

8. The priests used what to ask for magic to avoid rains at harvest time and to celebrate the refreshment of the earth mother goddess?
   a. the grand procession
   b. sacred chants
   c. a human sacrifice
   d. drum music

9. Which god was a sun god and the most powerful of all the Aztec gods?
   a. Tlaloc
   b. Huitzilopochtli
   c. Quetzalcoatl
   d. Tezcatlipoca

Constructed Response

10. Why did the Aztecs use human sacrifices? Who were usually sacrificed in the ceremonies? Use details from the reading selection to support your answer.

_____

_____

_____

_____

_____

The Aztec Calendar

The Lunar Calendar

The Aztecs, like the Mayas and ancient Egyptians, used two different calendars. The first calendar was similar to the one created by the Mayas and handed down through the ages. It was a **lunar calendar** based on the phases of the moon. The lunar calendar had 260 days. The Aztecs divided their calendar into 13 months, each having 20 days. They thought this calendar was magical. The priests used the lunar calendar to decide which days would be used for religious ceremonies and rituals. Priests also used this calendar to decide which days were lucky and should be used for important activities such as planting crops or going into battle.

The image of the sun god Tonatiuh is carved in the center of the Aztec calendar stone. Other carvings represent the Aztec days and religious symbols.

Day Names

A number of dots represented the months, and each of the 20 days had a name. Each of the days also had a **hieroglyph** (picture word). The days' names and their hieroglyphs are shown below:

Cipactli	Ehecatl	Calli	Cuetzpallin	Coatl
Crocodile	**Wind**	**House**	**Lizard**	**Serpent**

Miquiztli	Mazatl	Tochtli	Atl	Itzcuintli
Death's-head	**Deer**	**Rabbit**	**Water**	**Dog**

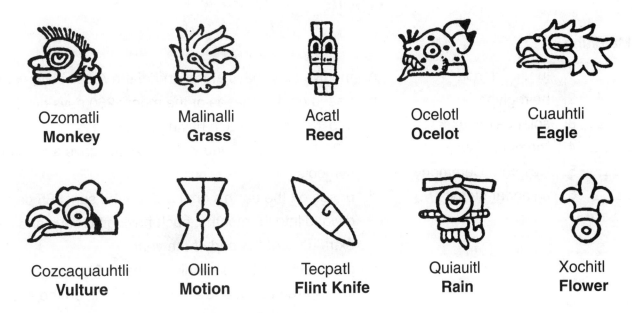

Ozomatli **Monkey**	Malinalli **Grass**	Acatl **Reed**	Ocelotl **Ocelot**	Cuauhtli **Eagle**
Cozcaquauhtli **Vulture**	Ollin **Motion**	Tecpatl **Flint Knife**	Quiauitl **Rain**	Xochitl **Flower**

Our New Year's day would have appeared on the Aztec calendar as:

(one dot = first month   crocodile = first day)

The Solar Calendar

The Aztecs established their second calendar on the movement of the sun. Similar to our calendar today, it had 365 days based on the time it took the earth to orbit the sun. They divided their **solar calendar** into 18 months, each containing 20 days. The extra five days were **"nothing" days** added to the end of each year. The Aztecs thought these five days were unlucky, so they did not give them names. The Aztec stopped all activities during the five "nothing" days. At the end of the five days, they gave a sacrificial victim in tribute to the gods.

Our calendar has centuries using 100-year divisions. Both of the Aztec calendars used 52-year divisions. The Aztecs had a major celebration at the start of each new 52-year cycle. Part of the celebration included the **New Fire Ceremony**. The priests extinguished the temple's altar fires, and the citizens let their household fires go out. At midnight of the new era, the priest would light a fire on the chest of a sacrificial victim. The people would then light a fire stick from the altar fire and use it to light their home fires.

One of the important artifacts from the Aztecs is the famous **calendar stone**. Discovered in 1790, the stone is about 12 feet in diameter and weights 20 tons. In the center of the stone is an image of the sun god Tonatiuh. Other carvings on the stone represent the Aztec days and religious symbols. Aztec priests may have placed the hearts of sacrificial victims on the stone's center during religious ceremonies.

Name: _____ Date: _____

Knowledge Check

Matching

_____ 1. lunar calendar

_____ 2. heiroglyph

_____ 3. solar calendar

_____ 4. "nothing" days

_____ 5. New Fire Ceremony

_____ 6. calendar stone

a. the five extra days at the end of the Aztec solar year

b. based on the phases of the moon; 260 days divided into 13 months, each having 20 days

c. a 20-ton stone carved with the Aztec days and religious symbols

d. based on the earth's orbit around the sun; 365 days divided into 18 months, each having 20 days and five extra days at the end of the year

e. celebration at the beginning of each 52-year cycle; all fires were put out and a new fire was lit on the altar

f. a picture word

Multiple Choice

7. Which calendar did the Aztecs use to decide when to plant crops or go into battle?

   a. the solar calendar

   b. the stellar calendar

   c. the Julian calendar

   d. the lunar calendar

8. What is the name of the 18th day of the Aztec lunar month?

   a. Calli

   b. Quiauitl

   c. Tecpatl

   d. Tochtli

9. How many years were in the Aztec calendar division that was similar to our 100-year century?

   a. 52

   b. 36

   c. 365

   d. 260

Critical Thinking

10. How was the New Fire Ceremony similar to some of the things we do today to celebrate the new year? Use details from the reading selection to help support your answer.

_____

_____

_____

_____

_____

Name: _____ Date: _____

Explore: Aztec Calendar Activity

Create an Aztec calendar for this month in the space below. For each day, include the hieroglyph, the Aztec name, and the English definition. Use the examples given in this chapter. Since there were only 20 Aztec days, you will have to repeat the names and hieroglyphs or make up some new ones of your own. Perhaps you could make a bulletin board display of your calendar.

The City of Tenochtitlan

The great pyramid and double temple to the gods Huitzilopochtli and Tlaloc was the most impressive structure in the plaza of Tenochtitlan.

Tenochtitlan

The greatest city of the Aztecs was **Tenochtitlan**. The early settlers built the village on an island in **Lake Texcoco**. They chose the island since the lake protected them against attacks from the mainland.

Tlaltelolco

A twin village, **Tlaltelolco**, was on another island to the north. The natives soon built a bridge between the two villages, but the two villages then became rivals. After a short battle, Tenochtitlan defeated and absorbed Tlaltelolco.

City on a Lake

As the villages grew into a city, the people needed more land. They dug mud from the lake bottom and piled it into mounds. The city became criss-crossed by **canals**. Tenochtitlan reminded the Europeans of Venice. The canals became the major streets of the city. Soon three large earthen **causeways** linked the city to the mainland. These causeways became the major entrances into the city. The three causeways joined at the great plaza in the center of the city.

Units and Sections

Tenochtitlan had four major units. These units had a total of 20 sections. Each clan had its own section of the city that contained the houses and gardens of the clan members. Each clan also had its own temple and school.

The Great Plaza

The **great plaza** was in the center of the city. It measured 900 square feet (about 300 square meters) and had over 60 buildings. The most impressive structure in the plaza was the pyramid and **double temple** to the gods Huitzilopochtli and Tlaloc. It was over 200 feet tall.

Four other temples and the sacred ball court were built in the great plaza. Other buildings in the plaza included the home of the priest, the house of a military unit, and the great palace of the ruler Montezuma. A large market place and the now-famous calendar stone were also in the great plaza.

The Spanish in Tenochtitlan

The Spanish first arrived in Tenochtitlan in November 1519. Hernando Cortés led the Spanish invaders. Tenochtitlan amazed them when they entered. One of the men wrote that he thought what he saw was a dream. The population of the city when the Spanish arrived is estimated at between 200,000 and 300,000 people. It was larger than any city in Europe at the time.

Cortés and his men soon defeated the Aztecs, and Tenochtitlan became a Spanish city. It continued to change after the Spanish conquest. In the 1600s the Spanish drained the lake. Today Mexico's capital, Mexico City, lies on the ruins of Tenochtitlan. The Mexican president's palace is on the location that was once Montezuma's palace.

Name: _____   Date: _____

Knowledge Check

Matching

_____ 1. Tenochtitlan

_____ 2. Lake Texcoco

_____ 3. Tlaltelolco

_____ 4. canals

_____ 5. causeways

_____ 6. great plaza

_____ 7. double temple

a. ditches filled with water that became the major streets of Tenochtitlan

b. large open space in the center of the city with temples and other public buildings

c. the greatest city of the Aztecs

d. raised earthen streets that connected the city to the mainland

e. body of water where Tenochtitlan was built on an island

f. built on top of a pyramid to honor the gods Tlaloc and Huitzilopochtli

g. a twin village built on another island in the lake; defeated and absorbed by Tenochtitlan

Multiple Choice

8. What had its own temple and school in its own section in the city of Tenochtitlan?

   a. each priest

   b. each family

   c. each clan

   d. each army

9. How many people were likely in Tenochtitlan when the Spanish first arrived?

   a. 200,000 to 300,000

   b. 20,000 to 30,000

   c. 30,000 to 60,000

   d. 100,000 to 200,000

10. The Mexican president's palace is on the site of what Aztec ruler's palace?

   a. Cortés

   b. Montezuma

   c. Atahualpa

   d. Tlaloc

Constructed Response

11. How did the Aztecs build their city in the middle of a lake? Use details from the reading selection to help support your answer.

_____

_____

_____

_____

_____

_____

_____

Aztec Art

Two serpents form her head. She has claws instead of hands and feet. Her skirt consists of many twisting snakes, and she wears a necklace made of human hearts and hands. Coatlicue, a goddess of the earth, stands nine and one-half feet tall. This shocking sight is one of the most famous Aztec sculptures.

The best remaining examples of Aztec art are its **architecture** and **sculpture**. Aztec sculpture remains among the most elaborate in the Americas. Almost all Aztec art used religious subjects and themes.

Aztec Temples

The temple was the most magnificent structure in each Aztec town. It was visible from miles away and stood on the top of huge pyramid structures. Great staircases rose up the sides of the pyramid. The great pyramid at Tenochtitlan had two temples at its peak.

This ceramic vessel is adorned with the image of Huehueteotl.

This serpent is made of inlaid turquoise.

Sculpture

Most of the sculpture came from decorations of the temple. The sculpture used a variety of subjects. Animals and representations of the gods were favorite subjects. We still can see examples of sculptures of spiders. Some of the sculpture is huge, like the calendar stone weighing over 20 tons, and some is very small and delicate.

The Aztecs used a variety of material for their sculpture. Stone was the most often used material. However, examples of Aztec art remain that were made of wood, jade, turquoise, emerald, and volcanic glass.

The Aztecs also made items of metal. They used metals easily found in nature. They did not know how to use iron or how to mix metals for great strength. Aztec workers used stone instead of metal tools. The craftsmen shaped gold, copper, and some silver into beautiful jewelry and decorations. Most of the Aztec gold treasures no longer exist. After conquering the Aztecs, Cortés and the Spaniards took the gold art works to Europe. The king of Spain had the treasures melted down to reuse the gold.

Pottery

Aztec craftsmen also made clay **pottery**. Some of it was plain and for everyday use. The Aztec kitchens contained many clay jars and other utensils. They also created elaborate and brightly colored ritual pottery.

Weaving

Aztec women spent much of their time **weaving** cloth. They dyed, embroidered, and decorated the cloth. The higher a person's social status, the more elaborate the decorations that appeared on his clothing. The Aztecs also excelled at feather weaving. Weavers raised exotic birds in cages to get brightly colored feathers. The weavers attached the feathers to a net to make cloaks, headdresses, and other decorative items. Only one example of Aztec feather weaving survives today. A headdress given by Montezuma to Cortés is preserved in a museum in Vienna.

Name: _____ Date: _____

Knowledge Check

Matching

_____ 1. architecture

_____ 2. sculpture

_____ 3. pottery

_____ 4. weaving

a. the art or practice of designing and contructing buildings

b. forming cloth by interlacing strands of fiber

c. carving or forming shapes out of hard substances

d. pots and other objects formed out of clay

Multiple Choice

5. Most Aztec sculpture was used to decorate what?

    a. homes

    c. the temple

    b. the streets

    d. the palace

6. Almost all Aztec art used what kind of subjects and themes?

    a. plants

    c. ordinary people

    b. religious

    d. the stars

7. What kind of artwork was melted down by the Spanish?

    a. gold

    c. wax

    b. stone

    d. jade

8. The only surviving example of Aztec feather weaving was given to whom by Montezuma?

    a. the king of Spain

    c. Columbus

    b. Pizarro

    d. Cortés

9. How did people get to the temples on the top of the great pyramid at Tenochtitlan?

    a. inside staircase

    c. elevator

    b. outside staircase

    d. hauled up by ropes

Constructed Response

10. Describe the sculpture of Coatlicue. Use details from the reading selection to help support your answer.

_____

_____

_____

_____

_____

_____

_____

Aztec Games

Ball Games

Tlachtli became the most important Aztec game. Tlachtli was a ball game similar to a Mayan game named **pok-a-tok**. Tlachtli began as a sport and later became a ritual game. The Aztecs played it during religious ceremonies. They played the game as entertainment for the ruler and priests as well as for the common people. Sometimes, the Aztecs sacrificed the losers to the gods.

We do not know the rules of the Mayan game, but all large Mayan and Aztec cities had game courts. The Mayan city **Chichén Itzá** had seven game courts. The largest court was 545 feet long and 225 feet wide. A basket was at each end of the court. The Mayas decorated the basket as a snake. It was 35 feet high.

The Aztec courts were similar to the Mayan courts. They were often near the temple areas. The courts were in the shape of a capital "I". They had seats on both sides for viewers. A vertical stone ring was in the middle of the side walls. The object of the game was to put the ball through the ring. A team also scored a point if the other team let the ball touch the ground.

Tlachtli used a hard rubber ball about six inches in diameter. The players wore padding. They could not touch the ball with their hands. The ball could only be moved by the players' hips, knees, legs, and elbows.

Board Games

The Aztecs also played board games. The most popular was *patolli*. It was similar to parcheesi or backgammon. However, we do not know the exact rules of patolli. The Aztecs played it on a cross-shaped design painted on a board or mat. They used beans painted with dots as dice. They used beans or kernels of **maize** (corn) as markers. The object of the game was to move around the board and return to home base. The Aztec often played patolli as a **gambling** game. The Aztec ruler Montezuma and the Spanish conqueror Cortés may have played patolli while Montezuma was a captive.

Tlachtli was an Aztec game played on a court like this. It seems to have been similar to a combination of modern basketball and soccer.

Name: _____ Date: _____

Knowledge Check

Matching

_____ 1. tlachtli

_____ 2. pok-a-tok

_____ 3. Chichén Itzá

_____ 4. patolli

_____ 5. maize

_____ 6. gambling

a. a game with a cross-shaped design painted on a board or mat

b. corn

c. a Mayan ball game played on a court

d. an Aztec ball game played on a court

e. betting money or property on the outcome of a game

f. Mayan city with seven game courts

Multiple Choice

7. To what modern games was tlachtli most similar?

   a. basketball and soccer
   c. bowling and horseshoes

   b. tennis and golf
   d. baseball and lacrosse

8. The Aztecs played tlachtli during what kinds of events?

   a. battles
   c. religious ceremonies

   b. feasts
   d. funerals

9. Aztec players could NOT touch the ball with what part of their bodies?

   a. legs
   c. knees

   b. elbows
   d. hands

Critical Thinking

10. Why do you think Montezuma and Cortés might have played patolli even though Montezuma was a prisoner? Use details from the reading selection and what you know about playing games to help support your answer.

_____

_____

_____

_____

_____

Name: _____ Date: _____

Aztec Games: Explore

    On this page is a drawing of the ancient Aztec board game patolli. You could make a larger drawing of the board on another piece of paper. The Aztecs used beans marked with dots as dice. They used beans or kernels of maize as markers.

    We do not know the rules of the Aztec game. Make up your own game rules. Perhaps you could have a patolli tournament.

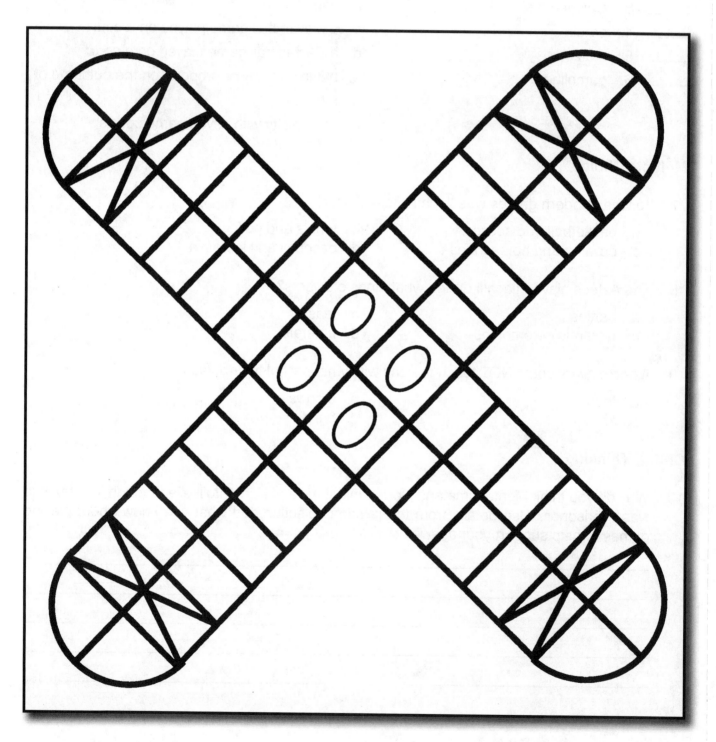

Aztec Agriculture

Planting Sticks

Aztec methods of farming were similar to those of the Mayan and Incan tribes. The Aztecs used a pointed stick to plant the crops. One person would make a hole in the ground with the stick. Another person would put the seeds in the hole and then cover the seeds with soil. The Aztecs never invented a plow to turn the earth.

Slash and Burn

The **slash and burn** method of agriculture was used by the Aztecs. They chopped down forest areas and left the trees and brush to dry in the heat of the sun for many days. The farmers then burned the areas to clear them. The ashes of the burnt trees provided fertilizer. The farmers then planted the new crops in the clearings.

The Aztecs created more farmland by forming small islands called chinampas in swamps and lakes.

Chinampas

Chinampas were the most interesting development of Aztec agriculture. Chinampas were small islands formed in lake and swamp areas. The farmers made them by digging the mud at the bottom of the lake or swamp and piling it into little mounds or islands. The Aztecs then planted crops and gardens on the chinampas. They are sometimes called floating gardens even though they did not really float.

The Aztec farmers also cut terraces into hillsides to create more farm land. They made many canals to help carry water to the fields.

Crops

Corn, called **maize** by the Aztecs, was the main crop. The Aztec farmers also grew avocados, as well as many varieties of beans, squash, sweet potatoes, and tomatoes. Different crops came from the lowlands. Major lowland crops included cotton, papayas, rubber, and cacao beans, from which chocolate is made.

Markets

After the harvest, farmers brought the crops to the marketplace in the nearest city. The Aztecs did not use animals or wheeled vehicles to move crops. The men carried everything to the market on their backs. In some of the distant villages, farmers used dugout canoes to move crops over rivers and canals.

The **market** was in the center of each town. Some of the markets were very large. The market in the city of Tlaltelolco was the largest. The Spaniard Hernando Cortés wrote that over 60,000 persons visited the market each day.

The Barter System

The Aztecs, like other Indian tribes, did not use money. They used a barter system. **Barter** is trading objects rather than buying and selling them. The markets contained many other things for barter besides food. Other items traded included weapons, animals, household goods, rare colorful feathers, and even slaves.

Name: _____ Date: _____

Knowledge Check

Matching

_____ 1. slash and burn

_____ 2. chinampas

_____ 3. maize

_____ 4. market

_____ 5. barter

a. method of agriculture where trees were chopped down, left to dry, and then burned

b. place where crops and other items were traded; in the center of each town

c. Aztec name for corn

d. small islands formed in lakes or swamps to provide land for crops and gardens

e. trading objects rather than buying and selling them

Multiple Choice

6. What ways did the Aztecs get their crops to the marketplace?
   a. packed on llamas
   b. hauled in wagons
   c. hauled in canoes
   d. carried on their backs

7. How did the ash from the slash and burn method help farmers?
   a. It was used to make houses.
   b. It provided fertilizer.
   c. It was used as food for animals.
   d. It made a soft surface to sleep on.

8. Which of these crops could not be grown in the higher altitudes of mountain regions?
   a. cacao
   b. squash
   c. maize
   d. beans

9. What was the main use of an Aztec planting stick?
   a. measuring where to put the seeds
   b. drawing garden plans
   c. making holes for the seeds
   d. scaring away birds

Constructed Response

10. Why did the Aztecs not need money? Use details from the reading selection to help support your answer.

_____

_____

_____

_____

_____

Aztec Warfare

Warfare was an important part of Aztec life. Every able-bodied Aztec man participated in fighting. The Aztecs believed it was a religious duty to be a warrior.

Aztec warriors were armed with slings, javelins, clubs, bows and arrows, and swords called macuahuitls. Warriors also carried shields decorated with paint and feathers.

Training for War

At the age of about 13, Aztec boys attended a school named the **telpuchalli**. At this school, the boys learned how to use weapons and the basics of warfare. Each boy would follow an experienced warrior into battle.

Taking Captives

It was important for the warrior to take **captives**. The Aztec honored the men who took many captives. The successful warriors often received social rank, land, or important offices as their reward.

Weapons

Aztec warriors used many weapons. The **macuahuitl** was the most important. It was a sword edged with sharp pieces of obsidian glass. The Aztecs also used bows and arrows, javelins, clubs, and slings.

Protective Clothing

The warriors carried shields and wore padded cotton armor. They decorated the shield with paint and feathers. They also wore brightly colored feather headdresses. They did not have uniforms. Each warrior dressed as he wished. They often had the sign of their group on their shield. The main warrior groups were the Order of the Eagle, the Order of the Jaguar, and the Order of the Arrows.

Battles

Battles did not last long. They did not use animals to carry supplies. The soldiers had to carry all of their supplies, so they did not have enough food and weapons to support a long attack. Most of the fighting was **hand-to-hand combat**. The first tribe to retreat was the loser.

The Aztecs went to war for two main reasons. They fought to get tribute and the needed supply of sacrificial victims for religious ceremonies. The tribe that lost the battle had to give the winning tribe gold, jewels, crops, and other valuable items. **Tribute** was everything the losing tribe had to give to the winning tribe. Often, the losing tribe paid tribute each year for many years after the battle. Tribute from many defeated tribes helped keep the Aztecs strong and powerful.

The goal of Aztec warfare was to capture rather than kill the enemy. Members of the losing tribe became slaves or sacrifices. Aztec religion demanded many human sacrifices to please the gods.

Name: _____ Date: _____

Knowledge Check

Matching

_____ 1. telpuchalli

_____ 2. captives

_____ 3. macuahuitl

_____ 4. hand-to-hand combat

_____ 5. tribute

a. an Aztec sword edged with sharp pieces of obsidian glass

b. a school attended by Aztec boys of age 13 where they learned the basics of warfare

c. everything the losing tribe had to give to the winning tribe

d. those taken prisoner during warfare; often used as slaves or sacrifices

e. fighting close enough for the warriors to come in contact

Multiple Choice

6. Which was NOT one of the main Aztec warrior groups?
   a. Order of the Eagle
   b. Order of the Jaguar
   c. Order of the Arrows
   d. Order of the Falcon

7. Why didn't battles last for a long period of time?
   a. They couldn't carry many supplies.
   b. They did not want to fight.
   c. They didn't have many weapons.
   d. Other tribes were too scared to fight.

8. Which warriors were the most honored?
   a. Those who took the most captives.
   b. Those who killed the most.
   c. Those who took the most loot.
   d. Those who died in battle.

9. What kept the Aztecs strong and powerful for many years?
   a. gold from Aztec mines
   b. the macuahuitl
   c. tribute from defeated tribes
   d. human sacrifice

Constructed Response

10. Why did the Aztecs want to capture rather than kill their enemies? How did they reward those warriors who took many captives? Use details from the reading selection to help support your answer.

_____

_____

_____

_____

_____

_____

_____

The Arrival of the Spaniards

Expeditions Into Mexico

Soon after Columbus landed in the Americas in 1492, the Spanish began settlements in the "new world." The Spanish governor of Cuba sent expeditions into Mexico in 1517 and 1518. **Hernando Cortés** headed the third expedition in 1519. They were looking for riches and slave labor for the plantations in Cuba. Cortés and his men, known as **Conquistadors**, encountered the Aztecs.

When Montezuma II met Cortés, he thought the Spaniard was the god Quetzalcoatl returning from across the sea, so he did not oppose the Spanish.

Conquering the Aztecs

Cortés and his men conquered the Aztecs in just three years. Many other tribes helped Cortés defeat the Aztecs. These tribes resented the heavy taxes they had to pay to the Aztecs.

The Aztec god Quetzalcoatl

The great Aztec chief **Montezuma II** did not oppose the Spaniards. He remembered an Aztec legend that said that the powerful god Quetzalcoatl had sailed across the sea and would return someday. Montezuma had never seen white men before. The metal armor of the Spanish also impressed him. Montezuma thought Cortés represented the returning god. Since he offered no resistance, the Spanish took Montezuma prisoner.

In 1520, the Aztecs rebelled against the invaders and drove the Spanish from the city of Tenochtitlan. By May 1521, Cortés and his men returned. They began a bloody attack against the Aztecs. Montezuma died from wounds he received in the attack. The next Aztec ruler, Cuauctemoc, surrendered to the Spanish in August 1521.

Destroying the Aztec Culture

The Spanish conquerors destroyed the Aztec cities. They made the Aztecs their slaves. The conquistadors took the Aztecs' gold and other treasures and sent them to Spain. Later, Spanish **missionaries** arrived. They destroyed Aztec temples and wiped out all traces of the Aztec religion. The religion of the white man soon replaced the old Aztec beliefs.

The Aztecs had little chance against the invaders. The Spanish had better weapons and armor than the natives. The Spanish also brought a new disease called **smallpox** with them from Europe. The natives did not have any resistance to this new infection. Thousands of Aztecs, including warriors, died from the disease.

After defeating the Aztecs, the Spanish invaders fought the Incas and the Mayas. The Spanish defeated the Incas in 1533. The last city of the Mayas fell in March 1697. The Spanish now had full control of the region.

Name: _____ Date: _____

Knowledge Check

Matching

_____ 1. Hernando Cortés

_____ 2. Conquistadors

_____ 3. Montezuma II

_____ 4. missionaries

_____ 5. smallpox

a. religious people who go into a foreign country to convert the natives to their religion; usually Christian

b. Spanish soldiers who conquered the natives of the new world

c. leader of the 1519 and later expeditions into Mexico that conquered the Aztecs

d. deadly disease brought by the Spanish for which the Aztecs had no resistance

e. ruler of the Aztecs at the time of the Spanish invasion

Multiple Choice

6. Who sent expeditions into Mexico?
   a. the French king
   b. the Spanish governor of Cuba
   c. the Spanish king
   d. the English governor of Virginia

7. Montezuma II thought the white men with metal armor represented what?
   a. the return of Montezuma I
   b. soldiers of the king of Spain
   c. the return of the god Quetzalcoatl
   d. an attack by a distant tribe

8. Who helped the Spanish defeat the Aztecs?
   a. other native tribes
   b. the French
   c. the Portuguese
   d. missionaries

9. Who was the last native group to be defeated by the Spanish?
   a. the Cubans
   b. the Incas
   c. the Aztecs
   d. the Mayas

Constructed Response

10. How did the spread of smallpox help the Spanish defeat the Aztecs? Use details from the reading selection to help support your answer.

_____

_____

_____

_____

_____

_____

Glossary

365-day calendar – (see solar calendar)

achiote – a tree that was used for brilliant red dye

adobe – a brick made of sun-dried earth and straw; used for building Aztec homes

agriculture – planting and harvesting crops and raising livestock

Ah Puch – Mayan god of death

ahkin – Mayan priests who had knowledge of mathematics and astronomy; they tried to predict the future and performed religious sacrifices and medical rituals

alphabet – a writing system where each character stands for a letter

Altiplano – people believed to be descended from the Olmecs; built the city of Teotihuacan

Andes Mountains – mountain range that runs along the western edge of South America; home of the Incas

aqueducts – a structure for carrying flowing water, usually from a river or stream to other locations

archeologists – scientists who study the lives of ancient humans

architecture – the art or practice of designing and constructing buildings

aryballus – an Incan jar with a cone-shaped bottom that was used to store liquids

astronomy – studying the movements of the sun, moon, planets, and stars

Atahualpa – brother who won the Incan civil war and became the Inca; he was later executed by the Spanish

Avenue of the Dead – the main road in Teotihuacan; it connected three of the main temples

Aztlan – the region of north or northwest Mexico from which the Aztecs came

backstrap loom – a loom tied to a tree and a belt that went around the weaver's back

ball court – place where native people like the Mayans and Aztecs played a game that has similarities to modern basketball, soccer, and football

barter – the exchange of certain goods for others; trading one item for another rather than using money

Bering Strait land bridge – an exposed piece of land that once connected Siberia to Alaska

borla – the Incan crown

bronze – metal made by melting copper and tin together

Buluc Chabtan – Mayan god of war and human sacrifice

cacao – plant whose beans are used to make chocolate

calendar stone – a 20-ton stone carved with the Aztec days and religious symbols; found in Tenochtitlan

Calmecac – a special school to train priests

calpolli – an Aztec extended family group; clan; the word meant "big house"

canal – a ditch that is dug to drain water either toward or away from an area; a ditch filled with water that became a major street of Tenochtitlan

canoe – a narrow boat with both ends pointed that is usually moved by paddling

Capac Raimi – "the magnificent festival"; most important and elaborate of the Incan festivals; began the Incan year in December

captives – those taken prisoner during warfare; often used as slaves or sacrifices

caravans – groups of traders and slaves carrying goods, traveling together for safety

causeway – a raised road two to four feet above ground level; raised earthen street that connected Tenochtitlan to the mainland

cavalry – soldiers mounted on horses

Ceneteotl – Aztec god of corn

Chac – Mayan rain god

chacas – the Incan name for their bridges

Chalchihuitlicue – Aztec goddess of lakes and rivers; Our Lady of the Turquoise Skirt

Chichén Itzá – ruins of this Mayan city include a great pyramid, observatory tower, sacred well, and ball courts

chicle – comes from the gum tree and is used in chewing gum

Chicomecoatl – Aztec goddess of crops

chinampas – small islands formed in lakes or swamps to provide land for crops and gardens

chosen women – group of women who lived in the temples and wove the finest wool into garments for the Incan ruler

chuñu – the Incan name for freeze-dried potatoes

city-state – an independent government unit formed around a city

clan – a group of extended Aztec families

classic era – period when the Mayas built many great cities

coastal highway – an Incan road that was 2,520 miles long; ran from the village of Tumbes in the north, through the desert, then into Chile

codex – the name for a Mayan book

Conquistadors – Spanish soldiers who conquered the natives of the new world, including the Incas, Aztecs, and Mayas

Copán – second largest Mayan city; its most famous ruin is the great staircase

cotton – a plant whose fibers can be spun into thread

council – a group with members from each Aztec tribe who chose a chief, enforced the laws, and punished wrongdoers

Court of a Thousand Columns – a plaza in Chichén Itzá where a large market was set up

coya – the main wife of the Inca or the Inca's sister

Cuzco – the capital city of the Incan empire

divining – studying objects to find magic signs

double temple – built on top of the great pyramid in Tenochtitlan to honor the gods Tlaloc and Huitzilopochtli

droughts – long periods without rain

dyes – substances that give color to cloth or other materials

eclipse – when the sun or moon is blocked by another heavenly body and its light does not shine on Earth

Ek Chaub – Mayan god of trade

embroidery – fancy stitching sewn on cloth

epidemic – an outbreak of disease that affects a large number of people at the same time

fertilizer – substance that makes soil more able to produce crops

ficus tree – the Mayas used fibers from the bark of this plant to make paper

fortress – a large structure built of stone where Incan citizens would gather in times of danger

Francisco Pizarro – leader of the Spanish soldiers who conquered the Incas

fresco – a painting done on a wall while the surface is still wet

gambling – betting money or property on the outcome of a game

geometric – designs based on simple shapes, such as straight lines, circles, or squares

glyphs – a writing system where pictures and symbols represent ideas and sounds; picture words

grand procession – a parade of young Aztec men from each clan and special warrior groups

great plaza – the large open space in Tenochtitlan in the center of the city with temples and other public buildings

halach uinic – ruler of a Mayan city-state; meant "the true or real man"; also may have been a high priest

hand-to-hand combat – fighting close enough for the warriors to come in contact

heiroglyph – a picture word

hematite – glass-like metal substance created by volcanic eruptions

Hernando Cortés – leader of the 1519 and later expeditions into Mexico that conquered the Aztecs

horizontal loom – a loom that was stretched about a foot off the ground between wooden supports

huaca – a sacred place or thing worshipped by the Incas

Huitzilopochtli – Aztec sun god and god of war; chief god of the city of Tenochtitlan

Huscar – brother who lost the Incan civil war

Inca – word meaning "the children of the sun god Inti," the ruler of the Incan empire, and the people of this civilization

indigo – a plant that was used for blue dye

Inti – the Incan sun god

Inti Raimi – Incan festival in June to celebrate the sun

irrigation – bringing water to dry land

Itzamná – Mayan head god; lord of the heavens; lord of night and day

Ix Chel – Mayan moon and rainbow goddess; goddess of weaving and childbirth

Kinich Ahau – Mayan sun god; god of the Mayan rulers

Knights of the Eagle – one group of Aztec warriors with special rank and privileges; wore feathers to represent their mascot

Knights of the Jaguar – one group of Aztec warriors with special rank and privileges; wore animal skins to represent their mascot

La Venta – Olmec city with a volcano-shaped pyramid

labor tax – (see **work tax** or **mita**)

Lake Texcoco – body of water where Tenochtitlan was built on an island

litter – a canopy-covered chair on a platform on which the Inca was carried

lunar calendar – Aztec calendar based on the phases of the moon; 260 days divided into 13 months, each having 20 days; also the sacred calendar of the Mayas used to plan religious events; the Mayan calendar did not have months

Machu Picchu – the best preserved Incan city; rediscovered in 1911

macuahuitl – an Aztec sword edged with sharp pieces of obsidian glass

maguey – fibers from this plant were used to weave the cable for Incan bridges; also used to make clothing for poorer Aztecs

maize – a native name for corn

man power – human strength or effort without the help of machines

Manco Capac – according to myth, the first Incan created by the sun god

market – place where crops and other items were traded; in the center of each town

Mayapan – the new Mayan capital in the 13th century

Mayas – people who lived in the Yucatan Peninsula and what is today Belize, El Salvador, Honduras, and Guatemala

Mictlantecuhli – Aztec god of the dead

missionaries – religious people who go into a foreign country to convert the natives to their religion; usually Christian

mita – the work or service tax all Incas had to pay to the government

Montezuma I – the greatest Aztec emperor; ruled from 1440 to 1468/9

Montezuma II – Aztec emperor during the empire's peak; ruled from 1502 until 1521 when he was killed during a battle between the Aztecs and the Spanish

mural – a large painting done on a wall

Nahuatl – the language spoken by the Aztecs

New Fire Ceremony – Aztec celebration at the beginning of each 52-year cycle; all fires were put out and a new fire was lit on the altar

"nothing" days – the five extra days at the end of the Aztec solar year; considered unlucky

observatory – place where native people studied the heavens

Ochpaniztli – the festival of the eleventh month to honor Tlazolteotl, the earth mother goddess

Olmec – name that means "rubber people"; they lived in central and southern Mexico

Paleo-Indians – the first people to settle in what is now North, Central, and South America

papa – the Incan name for potatoes

patolli – an Aztec board game played on a cross-shaped design painted on a board or mat

Pauca Huaray – Incan festival in March that celebrated the ripening of the earth

peasants – the poor people who worked the land

pedestrians – people who walk from place to place

plaza – a large open area in a city for public use; may contain a temple and be surrounded by other public buildings

pok-a-tok – a Mayan game played on a ball court, similar to tlachtli

polar ice caps – water frozen in the Arctic and Antarctic regions

post-classic era – period after the collapse of the Mayan empire

pottery – pots and other objects formed out of clay

ppolm – the Mayan name for merchants

pre-classic era – period when the Mayas lived in fishing villages along the Pacific Ocean and Caribbean Sea

pulp – tree fibers pounded into a soft mass that, when dried, forms paper

Pyramid of the Moon – smaller pyramid in Teotihuacan

Pyramid of the Sun – most famous structure in Teotihuacan; 200-foot-tall pyramid

Quetzalcoatl – Aztec god of learning and the priesthood; also god of arts and crafts; a peaceful god of the Toltecs, represented by a feathered snake

quipu – a knotted and colored cord device used for counting by the Incas

ransom – a payment given in exchange for the release of someone held captive

Royal Road – an Incan road that was 3,250 miles long; went from the northern border of the Incan empire through Ecuador, Peru, and Bolivia into Argentina and Chile

ruins – the remains of something that has been destroyed

sacred calendar – (see **lunar calendar**)

sacrifices – things given to the gods, such as valuable gifts, their own blood, or other humans

San Lorenzo – oldest known Olmec city where giant stone heads were found

sara – the Incan name for corn

sculpture – carving or forming shapes out of hard substances

shellfish – an invertebrate water animal with a shell, such as a clam, oyster, shrimp, or crab; used to make a deep purple dye

slash and burn – method of farming where trees are cut down, left to dry, and burned to clear land and provide fertilizer for the soil

smallpox – a deadly disease brought by the Europeans to which the natives had no resistance

solar calendar – Aztec calendar based on the earth's orbit around the sun; 365 days divided into 18 months, each having 20 days, with five extra days at the end of the year; also the 365-day calendar of the Mayas

Spanish conquest – time when soldiers from Spain conquered the natives of the new world

spinning – twisting fiber into yarn or thread

stela – a carved stone slab

tampus – rest houses every 12 to 20 miles along Incan roads

Tayasal – the last Mayan kingdom; conquered by the Spanish in 1697

Telpuchcalli – an Aztec school sponsored by a family calpolli; boys and girls attended starting at about age 13; many subjects were taught, including history, citizenship, arts and crafts, warfare, singing, and dancing

Temple of Quetzalcoatl – building in Teotihuacan named for the serpent god; carvings of serpents and a god name Tlaloc cover its walls

Temple of the Jaguars – building in Teotihuacan famous for its brightly colored wall murals

Tenochtitlan – the Aztec capital city; greatest Aztec city; built on Lake Texcoco

Teotihuacan – the capital of the Altiplano tribe; ancient city located near Mexico City

terraces – ridges cut into the steep sides of mountains to create more level farm land

Tezcatlipoca – Aztec sun god; most powerful of all gods; chief god of the city of Texcoco; a war-loving god of the Toltecs

thatched – covered with plant material, such as straw

The Well of Sacrifice – place where the Mayas threw live men to please the gods; located in Chichén Itzá

Tikal – the largest and perhaps oldest Mayan city

tlachti – a fast-moving Aztec game with a rubber ball; played on a ball court

Tlaloc – Aztec rain god; most important to farmers

Tlaltelolco – a twin village built on another island in Lake Texcoco; defeated and absorbed by Tenochtitlan

Tlazolteotl – the Aztec earth mother goddess; mother of the gods

Toltecs – people who became the most important tribe in the region after the Mayas left; settled in central Mexico and were powerful from A.D. 900 to 1200

Tonatiuh – an Aztec sun god

Topiltzin – a peaceful ruler of the Toltecs who founded the city of Tula

tortilla – Spanish name for Aztec cornmeal pancakes

trapezoid – a four-sided shape with the top smaller than the bottom; the shape of Incan door and window openings

tribe – a group made up of 20 Aztec clans

tribute – everything the losing tribe had to give the winning tribe

Tula – the capital and largest city of the Toltecs

Uma Raimi – Incan festival in October to celebrate water

Valley of Mexico – the region in central Mexico where the Aztecs settled

vertical loom – a loom attached to a wall; the weaver would stand to use it

Virachocha – the Incan god of nature; the creator; main god of the Incas

weaving – forming cloth by interlacing strands of fiber, such as yarn, reeds, vines, or feathers

work tax – the requirement that all Incas had to give a certain amount of their labor to the government; mita

Xipe Totec – Aztec god of spring, planting, and re-growth

Xiuhtecuhtli – an ancient Aztec fire god

Yucatan Peninsula – area of land that juts out into the Caribbean Sea; includes part of Mexico, Belize, and Guatemala

Yun Kaax – Mayan god of maize (corn); god of all agriculture

zero – the idea of using a symbol to represent the absence of all quantity

Answer Keys

The Arrival of Man
Knowledge Check (p. 2)
Matching
1. b 2. a 3. e 4. d
5. c
Multiple Choice
6. b, c 7. c 8. a 9. d
Constructed Response
10. Archeologists can look in ancient dumps to find information about what foods were eaten. Remains of stone spearheads, arrowheads, and tools give clues about the natives' lives. Stones used to grind grain and bits of broken pottery tell about early agriculture.
Map Follow-Up (p. 3)
Teacher check map.

The Olmecs
Knowledge Check (p. 5)
Matching
1. a 2. c 3. e 4. b
5. d
Multiple Choice
6. c 7. a 8. b 9. d
Constructed Response
10. We know the Olmecs had a form of picture writing. They had a number system and a calendar. They produced works of art, such as small carved pieces of jade and giant stone heads. They had ground mirrors of polished hematite. They harvested sap from rubber trees.

Teotihuacan
Knowledge Check (p. 7)
Matching
1. g 2. e 3. f 4. h
5. b 6. a 7. c 8. d
Multiple Choice
9. b 10. c
Constructed Response
11. The Altiplano made a special type of thin orange pottery. Examples of this pottery have been found throughout Mexico. This means the Altiplano traveled over a wide area and traded their goods with many other tribes.

The Mayas
Knowledge Check (p. 9)
Matching
1. g 2. d 3. e 4. a
5. f 6. c 7. b
Multiple Choice
8. c 9. b 10. d
Constructed Response
11. The Mayas had large cities. Tikal had 100,000 people or more. They built majestic pyramid temples. They improved methods of agriculture. They developed advanced mathematics and astronomy. They had a system of writing.
Map Follow-Up (p. 10)
Teacher check map.

Mayan Religion
Knowledge Check (p. 14)
Matching
1. e 2. g 3. f 4. c
5. d 6. a 7. b
Multiple Choice
8. c 9. a 10. d
Constructed Response
11. If the person survived, the priests would pull the sacrificed person out of the well. They were asked what messages they brought back from the gods. It was thought the gods had chosen to spare these victims. They were given special treatment from then on, since the Mayas believed they had spoken to the gods.

Mayan Cities
Knowledge Check (p. 16)
Matching
1. d 2. f 3. c 4. a
5. e 6. b 7. g
Multiple Choice
8. b 9. a 10. d
Constructed Response
11. In the center of the city, there was a large open plaza. Tall pyramids topped with temples were in the plazas. Public buildings, palaces, and ball courts surrounded the plazas. Rulers and priests lived in the city centers. The upper- and middle-class citizens built homes just outside the city center. Peasants lived in huts on the edges of the city. Raised roads, called causeways, ran through the city.

Mayan Writing
Knowledge Check (p. 18)
Matching
1. b 2. c 3. e 4. a
5. d
Multiple Choice
6. d 7. a 8. c
Constructed Response
9. The Spanish thought the Mayan books were evil. The Spanish were Christians, so they probably thought anything in the Mayan books would be about their heathen beliefs. They destroyed almost all of the Mayan books. This helped destroy the Mayan culture and allowed the Spanish to rule over them easier.

Mayan Mathematics and Astronomy: Knowledge Check (p. 20)
Matching
1. e 2. c 3. f 4. a
5. d 6. b
Multiple Choice
7. c 8. b 9. d
Constructed Response
10. The Mayas used their knowledge of astronomy and mathematics to predict eclipses and the orbit of the planet Venus. They developed a sacred calendar and a 365-day calendar. They also had a system of numbers that used a base of 20 and had a zero. The Mayan priests tried to predict events on earth by observing the heavenly bodies.
Explore: Mayan Math Exercise (p. 21)
Mayan Numbers:

0 = ⬭   2 = ● ●

4 = ●●●●   6 = ▬ ●

8 = ●●● ▬   9 = ●●●● ▬

11 = ● ▬▬   13 = ●●● ▬▬

14 = ●●●● ▬▬   15 = ▬▬▬

17 = ●● ▬▬▬   18 = ●●● ▬▬▬

1. ▬▬   2. ● ▬▬

3. ▬▬▬   4. ⬭

Student problems and answers will vary.

Mayan Arts and Crafts
Knowledge Check (p. 23)
Matching
1. e   2. b   3. a   4. c
5. d
Multiple Choice
6. c   7. a   8. d   9. b
Constructed Response
10. The Mayas used both vegetables and minerals for dyes. Black represented war. Yellow symbolized food. Red stood for blood. Blue indicated sacrifice.

Mayan Agriculture
Knowledge Check (p. 26)
Matching
1. d   2. b   3. e   4. a
5. f   6. c
Multiple Choice
7. a   8. d   9. c
Constructed Response
10. Slash and burn farming cleared the land for farming. The ashes provided fertilizer for the soil. This made the soil rich for a while. However, the soil wore out quickly. Fields would have to rest for two or three years before replanting. More fields would have to be cleared to make up for the land that had to rest.

Mayan Trade
Knowledge Check (p. 28)
Matching
1. c   2. a   3. e   4. d
5. b
Multiple Choice
6. d   7. c   8. a   9. c
Constructed Response
10. The Mayas traded fruits and vegetables, salt, honey, dried fish, cacao beans, turtle eggs, deer meat, and birds. They also traded non-food items, such as cotton cloth, animal skins, feathers, shells, gold, emeralds, jade, and other valuable stones. They also bought and sold slaves.

The Great Mayan Mystery
Knowledge Check (p. 30)
Matching
1. a   2. d   3. c   4. b
Fact/Opinion
5. O   6. F   7. O   8. O
9. F   10. O
Critical Thinking
11. Answers will vary.

The Mayas and the Spanish
Knowledge Check (p. 32)
Matching
1. d   2. b   3. e   4. a
5. c
Multiple Choice
6. c   7. b   8. d   9. b
Constructed Response
10. There were civil wars among the independent Mayan city-states. Droughts and hurricanes destroyed crops and homes. Epidemics of diseases killed thousands of Mayas. These things continued to weaken the Mayan tribes.

The Toltecs
Knowledge Check (p. 34)
Matching
1. f   2. e   3. b   4. a
5. d   6. c
Multiple Choice
7. a   8. b   9. d
Constructed Response
10. The Toltecs demanded tributes from the people whom they conquered. Many of the captives of war became human sacrifices to the gods.

Explore: The City of Tula Maze (p. 35)
Slight variations in the route are possible.

The Incas
Knowledge Check (p. 37)
Matching
1. c   2. a   3. d   4. f
5. e   6. b
Multiple Choice
7. c   8. a   9. b
Constructed Response
10. The Incas did not develop a system of writing, so they left no books or writings about their history. We can study the writings of the Spanish who conquered the Incas. We can also study Incan artifacts in the ancient cities to try to get clues about the early Incas.

Map Follow-Up (p. 38)
Teacher check map.

Incan Religion
Knowledge Check (p. 40)
Matching
1. b   2. a   3. d   4. c
Multiple Choice
5. b   6. d   7. a   8. c
9. a
Constructed Response
10. The Incas believed that their ruler was a son of the sun god Inti. Since

his father was a god, the ruler was a god too. He should be worshipped as a living god on Earth.

Incan Agriculture
Knowledge Check (p. 43)
Matching
1. d   2. c   3. a   4. b
5. e
Multiple Choice
6. d   7. c   8. a   9. d
Constructed Response
10. Modern Andes farmers still use many of the ancient Incan terraces. The Incan water system of canals, tunnels, and aqueducts is still in use today.

Incan Weaving
Knowledge Check (p. 45)
Matching
1. c   2. d   3. g   4. a
5. b   6. f   7. e
Multiple Choice
8. c   9. b   10. a
Constructed Response
11. First, wool was gathered from the animals. Then, the women dyed the wool. They spun the wool into thread. Next, they wove the thread into cloth. They used geometric patterns when weaving the cloth. The cloth might be decorated with embroidery or other items like gold, silver, copper, or feathers.

Incan Arts and Crafts
Knowledge Check (p. 47)
Matching
1. d   2. b   3. a   4. c
True/False
5. T   6. F   7. F   8. T
9. F   10. T
Constructed Response
11. The Incas used gold and silver to make masks, plates, and jewelry. They also used copper, tin, and bronze to make knives, weapons, pins for garments, and tools. Pottery included three-legged pots, plates, and drinking cups. The aryballus was used to store liquids.

Incan Roads and Bridges
Knowledge Check (p. 49)
Matching
1. e   2. b   3. c   4. a
5. f   6. d
Multiple Choice
7. b   8. d   9. c
Constructed Response
10. The rope fibers would stretch, which would lower the bridge over time. The fibers would also break down due to wear and tear and being out in the weather.

Cities of the Incas
Knowledge Check (p. 51)
Matching
1. c   2. a   3. e   4. d
5. b
Multiple Choice
6. b   7. c   8. d   9. c
Constructed Response
10. The Incas used huge blocks of stone. They cut and polished each stone with small stone tools. Then they moved each stone into the proper place. The stones fit together perfectly and did not need cement to hold them in place. The Incas used trapezoidal openings for the doors and windows. The four-sided openings were smaller at the top than at the bottom.

The Inca and His Government
Knowledge Check (p. 53)
Matching
1. a   2. d   3. c   4. b
5. e
Multiple Choice
6. a   7. c   8. b   9. d
Constructed Response
10. The Inca was worshipped as a god and ruler. He had absolute power. He had many wives and children. He wore a crown decorated with gold. His garments were made of the finest wool, and he only wore each garment once. The Inca ate and drank only from gold plates and goblets. He was carried in a gold litter under a gold canopy. A new palace was built for each Inca. His throne was gold. When he died, his body was mummified and put

in the old palace as a shrine where the mummy was worshipped.

The Incas and the Spanish Conquest: Knowlege Check (p. 55)
Matching
1. c   2. e   3. b   4. a
5. d
Multiple Choice
6. c   7. b   8. a   9. b
Critical Thinking
10. The Spanish saw how much gold and silver the Incas had. If it was easy for them to fill a prison cell with it, there must be plenty more. The Spanish would not be satisfied until they had conquered the Incas and taken all their riches.

The Aztecs
Knowledge Check (p. 58)
Matching
1. f   2. c   3. d   4. a
5. b   6. g   7. e
Multiple Choice
8. a   9. d   10. b
Constructed Response
11. Each Aztec city-state had its own government and distinct culture. Tenochtitlan, along with Texcoco, and Tlacopan, formed an alliance that became the Aztec empire. At one time, 489 cities paid tribute and taxes to the empire. The Aztecs did not try to unify the empire. Military units were stationed throughout the empire to maintain control. A great noble commanded each army and served as governor. A council of nobles chose the emperor from members of the royal family.

Map Follow-Up (p. 59)
Teacher check map.

Aztec Daily Life
Knowledge Check (p. 62)
Matching
1. d   2. a   3. e   4. b
5. f   6. c
Multiple Choice
7. d   8. a   9. d   10. c
Constructed Response
11. An Aztec boy would learn a craft from his father or other adult. He

would go with him to a workshop. The father would teach his son how to use tools to create the craft items. The boy would start helping with simple jobs and would eventually learn how to be a master craftsman.

Aztec Society
Knowledge Check (p. 64)
Matching
1. d   2. b   3. a   4. c
True/False
5. T   6. F   7. T   8. T
9. F   10. F   11. T
Constructed Response
12. The calpollis took care of the needs of their clan members. Land was owned by the calpolli and divided among its families. Extended families lived and worked together. Most decisions were made by popular vote. The calpollis ran schools to teach its children. The family arranged all marriages. Each tribe sent a leader to be on the council, so there was a voice for each tribe. The council took care of civil, religious, and war matters.

Aztec Religion
Knowledge Check (p. 67)
Matching
1. e   2. c   3. d   4. a
5. b
Multiple Choice
6. b   7. a   8. b   9. d
Constructed Response
10. The Aztecs believed the blood given in sacrifice gave the gods new strength and energy. The sacrifices were usually men who were either captives of war or slaves.

The Aztec Calendar
Knowledge Check (p. 70)
Matching
1. b   2. f   3. d   4. a
5. e   6. c
Multiple Choice
7. d   8. c.   9. a
Critical Thinking
10. Answers will vary but could include: It is similar to how we may get rid

of the old and bring in new things on the new year. We count down to midnight and then light a ball or set off fireworks.

The City of Tenochtitlan
Knowledge Check (p. 73)
Matching
1. c   2. e   3. g   4. a
5. d   6. b   7. f
Multiple Choice
8. c   9. a   10. b
Constructed Response
11. The Aztecs built Tenochtitlan on an island in Lake Texcoco. To create more land, they dug mud from the lake and piled it into mounds. Tenochtitlan defeated and absorbed the twin city of Tlaltelolco. They kept enlarging the land, and the city became criss-crossed by canals. They also built three large earthen causeways that linked the city with the mainland. The causeways joined at the great plaza in the center of the city.

Aztec Art
Knowledge Check (p. 75)
Matching
1. a   2. c   3. d   4. b
Multiple Choice
5. c   6. b   7. a   8. d
9. b
Constructed Response
10. The head of Coatlicue is formed by two serpents. She has claws instead of hands or feet. Her skirt is made of many twisting snakes. She wears a necklace made of human hearts and hands. The sculpture is nine and one-half feet tall.

Aztec Games
Knowledge Check (p. 77)
Matching
1. d   2. c   3. f   4. a
5. b   6. e
Multiple Choice
7. a   8. c   9. d
Critical Thinking
10. They might have played the game just to pass the time. They might have wanted to prove that one was

smarter than the other by seeing who had the best strategy in the game. They might have gambled on the outcome of the game to get something they wanted.

Aztec Agriculture
Knowledge Check (p. 80)
Matching
1. a   2. d   3. c   4. b
5. e
Multiple Choice
6. c, d   7. b   8. a   9. c
Constructed Response
10. The Aztecs used the barter system. They traded one item for another rather than buying and selling with money. They traded food, weapons, animals, household goods, feathers, and slaves.

Aztec Warfare
Knowledge Check (p. 82)
Matching
1. b   2. d   3. a   4. e
5. c
Multiple Choice
6. d   7. a   8. a   9. c
Constructed Response
10. The Aztecs wanted to use captives as slaves or human sacrifices. They were no good to the Aztecs if they were killed in battle. Warriors who took many captives were rewarded with social rank, land, or important offices.

The Arrival of the Spaniards
Knowledge Check (p. 84)
Matching
1. c   2. b   3. e   4. a
5. d
Multiple Choice
6. b   7. c   8. a   9. d
Constructed Response
10. The Aztecs had no resistance to smallpox. Thousands of Aztecs died from the disease. This included many warriors. The Aztec army and the rest of the population were weakened by the disease.

For Further Reading

For Older Readers:

Berdan, Frances F. *The Aztecs of Central Mexico: An Imperial Society*. Thomson/Wadsworth, 2005.

Bray, Warwick. *Everyday Life of the Aztecs*. Peter Bedrick Books, 1991.

Brunhouse, Robert L. *In Search of the Maya*. Ballantine Books, 1990.

Cameron, Ian. *Kingdom of the Sun God: a History of the Andes and their People*. Facts on File, 1991.

Coe, Michael D. *The Maya*, Seventh Ed. (Ancient Peoples and Places). Thames & Hudson, 2005.

Divan, Thomas J. *Aztecs and Mayas*, V1 (1909). Kessinger Publishing, LLC, 2010.

Everyday Life of the Incas (Everyday Life). Dorset House Publishing Co Inc., 1990.

Gruzinski, Serge. *The Aztecs: Rise and Fall of an Empire*. Harry N. Abrams, Inc., 1992.

Indians of the Andes: Aymaras and Quechuas. Routledge, 2004.

Jones, David. *The Inca World: Ancient People & Places*. Lorenz Books, 2010.

Morales, Demetrio S. *The Maya World*. Minutiae Mexicana Series, 2003.

Morris, Craig and Adriana von Hagen. *The Incas* (Ancient Peoples and Places). Thames & Hudson, 2011.

Sharer, Robert J. and Loa Traxler. *The Ancient Maya*, 6th Ed. Stanford University Press, 2005.

For Younger Readers:

Baquedano, Elizabeth. *Aztec, Inca & Maya* (DK Eyewitness Books). DK CHILDREN, 2005. (Ages 8+)

Kendall, Sarita. *The Incas* (Worlds of the Past). Crestwood House, 1992. (Ages 10+)

Newman, Sandra. *The Inca Empire* (True Books: Ancient Civilizations). Children's Press, 2010. (Ages 7+)

Perl, Lila. *The Ancient Maya* (People of the Ancient World). Children's Press, 2005. (Ages 10+)

Santella, Andrew. *The Aztec* (True Books: American Indians). Children's Press, 2003. (Ages 8+)

Shuter, Jane. *The Maya* (History Opens Windows). Heinemann-Raintree, 2008. (Ages 7+)

Sonnenborn, Liz. *The Ancient Aztecs* (People of the Ancient World). Children's Press, 2005. (Ages 10+)

Takacs, Stefanie. *The Inca* (True Books: American Indians). Children's Press, 2004. (Ages 8+)

Takacs, Stefanie. *The Maya* (True Books: American Indians). Children's Press, 2003. (Ages 7+)

Wood, Tim. *The Aztecs*, (See Through History). Viking Children's Books, 1992. (Grades 4 to 7)